Reforming Defense

• Reforming Defense
THE STATE OF AMERICAN CIVIL-MILITARY RELATIONS

David C. Hendrickson

THE JOHNS HOPKINS UNIVERSITY PRESS • BALTIMORE AND LONDON

© 1988 The Johns Hopkins University Press
All rights reserved
Printed in the United States of America

The Johns Hopkins University Press, 701 West 40th Street, Baltimore, Maryland 21211
The Johns Hopkins Press Ltd., London

The paper used in this publication meets the minimum requirements of American National Standard for Information Sciences — Permanence of Paper for Printed Library Materials, ANSI Z39.48-1984.

Library of Congress Cataloging-in-Publication Data

Hendrickson, David C.
  Reforming defense.

  Bibliography: p.
  Includes index.
  1. United States. Armed Forces. 2. United States — Military policy. 3. Civil-military relations — United States. I. Title.
UA23.H448   1988   355'.00973   87-17003
ISBN 0-8018-3550-X (alk. paper)

For My Mother and Father

For forms of government let fools contest
Whate'er is best administered is best.
                    ALEXANDER POPE

Nothing is more pitiful than the arrogant disdain of most of our contemporaries for questions of form, for the smallest questions of form have acquired in our time an importance which they never had before; many of the greatest interests of mankind depend upon them. I think that if the statesmen of aristocratic ages could sometimes despise forms with impunity and frequently rise above them, the statesmen to whom the government of nations is now confided ought to treat the very least among them with respect and not neglect them without imperious necessity. In aristocracies the observance of forms was superstitious; among us they ought to be kept up with a deliberate and enlightened deference.
                    ALEXIS DE TOCQUEVILLE

Contents

Preface and Acknowledgments xi
List of Abbreviations xiii
Introduction 1

PART I · AMERICAN CIVIL-MILITARY RELATIONS IN THEORY AND PRACTICE

1 · The Division of Responsibility 11

  Strategy, Operations, and Administration 11
  The Foundation of American Military Professionalism:
  Root and Mahan 17
  The Military Professional, Fusionism, and the
  Bureaucratic Revisionists 22

2 · The Lack of Unified Direction 29

  Congress and the Separation of Powers 30
  Servicism and the McNamara Revolution 34
  Strategic Pluralism and Presidential Leadership 42

3 · Some Organizational Dilemmas 46

  Centralized Oversight and Decentralized Initiative 46
  Expertise and Innovation 49
  The Burden of Proof 57

PART II · THE CALL FOR REFORM

4 · The Limitations of Military Reform 63

  The Nature of the Military Reform Movement 63
  Positive Contributions and General Themes 70
  The Doctrinal Debate, NATO Reform, and Ground Forces 75
  The Future of the Carrier Task Force 85

The Controversy over Air Power 91
Military Reform and Civil-Military Relations 97

5 · The Question of Institutional Reform 100
The Defense Budget Process 102
Elevating Purposive Organization 105
Rewriting the Key West Accord 108
JCS Reform 111
The Modest Virtues of Institutional Reform 116

Conclusion 119
Notes 125
Select Bibliography 139
Index 147

Preface and Acknowledgments

This work began in curious fashion. Setting out five years ago to study the implications of the military reform movement for the larger questions of American strategy, I became increasingly disturbed by the institutional implications of the reform project. The significance of the many defense reform movements that arose in the 1980s, I came to believe, could not be fully understood or evaluated without continual reference to the classic problems of civil-military relations. The understanding of civil-military relations, in turn, could not fail to be enhanced by seeing the subject in relation to the practical dilemmas of contemporary American military policy.

My debt to others who have written in this field is for the most part apparent in what follows, but the writings of one scholar — Samuel P. Huntington — were particularly formative and deserve mention here. Though I have come to disagree with Professor Huntington on a variety of matters, the theoretical categories he has employed to illuminate the character of civil-military relations I have found indispensable. A recent second reading of his book *The Soldier and the State*, first published in 1957, confirmed my initial impression that it is a landmark study in postwar American social science.

An early version of part of this book was presented at a seminar at the Lehrman Institute in December 1983. I dimly recall a scattering of generous comments; the critical ones, however, were far more abundant. The severest critics, I regret to say, often made the most telling points. They forced me to reconsider a number of themes and, in the end, to reconstruct entirely the architecture of the book. Among those who participated in the seminar, I would particularly like to thank Kenneth Adelman, Richard Challener, Eliot Cohen, James Fallows, David Gompert, Derek Leebaert, Barry Posen, and Richard Ullman for their perceptive observations. And I also thank Robert W. Tucker, Nicholas X. Rizopoulos, Michael Mandelbaum, and Linda Wrigley of the Institute for their generous support in this undertaking, as in others.

Thanks are due also to the Colorado College for making available the time to complete the book and for defraying various expenses associated with it. A legion of people at CC — Quincy Aragon, Edie Dulacki, Byron Freney, Katherine Herr, Deborah Houy, John Leigh, Helen Lynch, Lisa Peterson, and Becky Whitmer — have assisted me over the past three years, and it is a pleasure to record my thanks to them here. The reader for the Johns Hopkins University Press made a number of valuable suggestions in his review of the manuscript, and the book was expertly edited by Alice M. Bennett.

Two other people deserve my particular thanks. Curtis Cook gave generously of his time in reading many drafts of the manuscript and in providing me with critical comments, which proved of great utility in the revision of the book. W. Seth Carus, at an early stage of the project, filled me with ideas on a wide range of topics and set me on the right road. To both of them I am deeply indebted.

Abbreviations

ADC	Air Defense Command
AWACS	Airborne Warning and Control System
CAB	Civil Aeronautics Board
CNO	Chief of Naval Operations
CTOL	Conventional Takeoff and Landing
DIVAD	Division Air Defense Gun
FTC	Federal Trade Commission
ICBM	Intercontinental Ballistic Missile
ICC	Interstate Commerce Commission
IFV	Infantry Fighting Vehicle
JCS	Joint Chiefs of Staff
MAC	Material Airlift Command
NATO	North Atlantic Treaty Organization
PPBS	Planning, Programming, and Budgeting System
RDF	Rapid Deployment Force
SAC	Strategic Air Command
SUM	Shallow Underwater Missile
VSS	V/STOL Support Ship
V/STOL	Vertical/Short Takeoff and Landing

Reforming Defense

Introduction

The position of the military in American life has almost always been a difficult one. At the beginning of the nation's history the mere existence of standing armies was widely seen as necessarily destructive of a republican form of government, an attitude that persisted, though in different idioms, well into the twentieth century. Even when international peril in the 1940s and 1950s gave the uniformed military a more respected position in American life, a large residue of distrust remained, flowering again in the 1960s as a consequence of the war in Vietnam. In recent years a new critique has arisen, associated with the loosely affiliated group of writers who have come to be known as the "military reformers." Whereas previous critiques of the military often denied the necessity of military establishments and saw the profession of arms as morally depraved, the military reformers acknowledge by their very preoccupation with things military the legitimacy and necessity of thinking about the military art. Whereas previous critiques of the military in American life almost never accepted the military on its own terms, the military reformers have done so. But the residue of distrust remains. For it is the conviction of the military reformers that the American armed services have completely misjudged the character of contemporary warfare in the air, at sea, and on land. According to the reformers, it is precisely within the area of the military's professional function — a domain whose very existence was often denied by previous critics — that the services have most completely gone awry and are most in need of reform.

The critique of the military reformers centers on alleged deficiencies in doctrine, organization, force structure, manpower policy, and weapons acquisition. It includes the following propositions: (1) that the American military services continue to display a mistaken doctrinal emphasis on an attrition style of warfare and ought for basic reasons of strategy to prefer "maneuver warfare"; (2) that the weapons traditionally procured by the services do not work in combat and are expensive to maintain, from infantry fighting vehicles that are positively dangerous to the soldiers who occupy them to fighter aircraft (like the F-15) far less reliable and effective than the cheaper planes traditionally shunned by the Air Force; (3) that the operational concepts favored by the services are badly mistaken, from the Navy's emphasis on concentrating its combat power in rings around the large-deck aircraft carrier (so as to form a veritable bull's-eye for the enemy) to the Air Force's continued emphasis on interdiction deep in the enemy rear — a suicidal mission, given the dense array of surface-to-air missiles such invading aircraft would face in Warsaw Pact airspace, but one that is nevertheless heavily funded to the exclusion of more relevant capabilities, like close air support; and (4) that the personnel policies of the services reflect internal convenience rather than strategic need, maladies revealed in rotation policies that "punch tickets" but destroy cohesion in combat units and make impossible the development of real expertise in the administration of the services.

Alongside the call for military reform there has arisen a procedural critique of the military establishment — one focused on the institutional setting in which American defense policy is formulated and executed. Though many military reformers have joined in the latter critique, it is analytically distinct from "military reform" as such. Unlike the military reformers, whose practical achievements thus far have been paltry, the organizational reformers achieved a striking success with the passage, in 1986, of the Goldwater-Nichols Defense Reorganization Act. The critique on which that legislation was based held that serious deformations in the organization of the military services had led to a military establishment in which a parochial concern for the interests of each military service had eclipsed concern for the national interest. As previously organized, according to this view, the American military was incapable of offering badly needed strategic advice to its civilian superiors, and its operational planning was the product of compromises and logrolling that inevitably led to failures on the battlefield.

Many of the criticisms directed against the organization of the defense establishment are old ones; there has, in fact, never been widespread satisfaction with the organization of the U.S. military since World War II, or so at least one may judge from the numerous presidential commissions appointed to study the problem since the 1950s. Despite these efforts, though, there had been little change since the major reorganization of the Department of Defense in 1958 and the McNamara reforms of the early 1960s; the reports of the presidential commissions had gone unread, and their remedies had been resisted. This time, though, the result was different. In the 1980s the calls for organizational change gathered support in high places, particularly in the armed services committees in both houses of Congress. Although Secretary of Defense Caspar Weinberger and the Joint Chiefs of Staff professed themselves satisfied with existing arrangements and resisted the calls for organizational change, there came to exist an impressive intellectual case for far-reaching institutional reforms that attracted support all along the political spectrum. Whereas the military reformers are for the most part mavericks whose center of power lies outside the defense establishment, the organizational reformers comprise distinguished academicians, former Secretaries of Defense, retired military officers, leading congressmen, and other such luminaries — a coalition that succeeded in effecting significant change in 1986.

Whether the impulse for organizational reform has now been spent remains to be seen. Many are certain to be dissatisfied with how the organizational reforms work out in practice, and they will call for more sweeping changes in the future. Moreover, the agenda of the organizational reformers includes matters barely addressed in the 1986 legislation, two of which seem likely to receive renewed attention. One is the defense budget process, particularly the way Congress deals with military requests. Another is the organization of the executive branch, where there is an emphasis on "input" but not on "output" and on function rather than mission — tendencies, many critics hold, powerfully reinforced by structural inadequacies in the Department of Defense.

Alongside the calls for "military reform" and "organizational reform" there is a third set of proposals for change that may be classified as "administrative reform." Sparked by the spare-parts scandals that erupted in 1984, these proposals for reform center on the vast administrative machinery that supports the military establishment. Proposals to root out "waste, fraud, and abuse" are of course nothing new; indeed, charges of mismanagement and inefficiency predate the establishment of the Department of Defense, as do many of the remedies for dealing with them. Among the most notable of the latter are those that call for greater competition in the procurement of military equipment, the elimination of duplication among the services, testing bureaus within the Pentagon independent of the service commands responsible for developing weaponry, and the elimination of the "revolving door" whereby military officers retire to lucrative positions with the defense contractors they ostensibly supervise. In this area, more than the others, there are reformers drunk and sober — from scandalmongers who recall the muckrakers of the Progressive Era to conservative Republican businessmen who believe in the virtues of a free-market economy and would like to bring sound business practice to the Pentagon.

Many of these proposals for reform overlap and reinforce each other. It is the services' emphasis on "high-tech weaponry" and technological innovation that often makes costs so difficult to estimate: reducing emphasis on the one, on this view, would facilitate improvements in the other. Others argue that most "waste" and "duplication" stems from the separate administration of the three services: on this view, organizational reforms that brought about a more unified military viewpoint would help eliminate duplication and thus permit substantial savings in the administration of the services. Still, each set of reform proposals is different from the others, and they are by no means wholly consistent. Competition is certainly desirable in military procurement, but the result might be additional duplication — a dilemma posed by the congressional effort to force the Air Force to procure the F-20. Improving the administration of the services by strengthening the authority and improving the education of the military officers who manage procurement programs appears to be an unexceptionable idea — but officers so trained will come to resemble "managers" rather than "warriors," and it is not clear that this represents a net improvement. It is not only between these three areas of reform — military, organizational, and administrative — that we encounter trade-offs among competing options; within each of these fields opinion is by no means unanimous. Indeed, of defense reform it may fairly be said that though there is a consensus that we need it, there is no agreement on what it is.

"The history of Western political thought," Maurice Vile has written, "portrays the development and elaboration of a set of values — justice, liberty, equality, and the sanctity of property — the implications of which have been examined and debated down through the centuries; but just as important is the history of the debates about the institutional structures and procedures which are necessary if these values are to be realized in practice, and reconciled with each other."[1] A comparable distinction may be drawn with respect to the study of national security affairs. In this area as well, there are two levels of analysis — one concerned with the measures required to address threats external forces pose to the state's physical security, material well-being, or institutional integrity; the other — institutional policy — with the way these measures are formulated and executed.[2] "The values that characterize Western thought," Vile noted, "are not self-executing," and the same is true of the values that military policy is designed to serve. Certain institutional arrangements are required to give effect to these values — arrangements that will function effectively even without enlightened statesmen at the helm.

It is the principal assumption of this work that none of the three reform movements identified earlier can be fully understood or evaluated without continual reference to the classic problems of civil-military relations. This is obviously the case with the proposals for the reform of defense organization; unless we have some vision of the ideal character of civil-military relations as well as some grasp of their history, the reform of our institutions will inevitably be flat-footed or misconceived. But it is equally true of the other two sets of reform proposals. The efficiency with which the United States acquires its weapons and supports all the other activities indispensable to the functioning of the military is not merely a narrow problem for the administrative expert or the managerial consultant — though of course it can be and has been profitably studied from this point of view. Many of the greatest inefficiencies are deeply rooted in the process of defense decision making and in the complicated political relations that exist among the military services, defense contractors, and powerful congressmen — who as often as not are divided in outlook from the occupant of the White House.

The military reform movement raises a number of these institutional problems as well. Much, though not all, of the reform critique is concerned with matters that go to the heart of the military's professional function, yet this critique has assumed an important place in the debate over contemporary military policy because it enjoys the support of civilians. Many present and former members of the military services, to be sure, have contributed to the arsenal of reform argument. Yet it seems fair to say that the reform movement is predominantly civilian in character. Reform arguments enjoy their greatest popularity in the news media and the Congress. They have attracted the support of a number of politicians, including liberal Democrats such as Gary Hart and Edward Kennedy and conservative Republicans like Newt Gingrich and Jim Courter. But within the military services themselves — with the exception of some elements of the Marine Corps and the Army — preponderant opinion is decidedly out of sympathy with most reform ideas and seems likely to remain so. If the services are going to change their outlook on the matters the military reformers think most important, change will have to be forced upon them from the outside.

Such an enterprise, I believe, raises delicate questions in civil-military relations. Precisely because the matters in question lie so closely to the military's professional function, it is not an enterprise to be undertaken lightly. At the very least, the military reformers must meet a significant burden of proof — a heavier one than falls on organizational or administrative reformers, whose area of interest lies well within civilian purview. Even if the burden of proof is met, moreover, reform ought to be of a certain kind: it must proceed at least partly "from the inside" as well as "from the outside." Civilian reformers, in other words, must reach into the military itself and find officers convinced of the necessity of change and capable of effecting it. Civilians have a right to get rid of incompetents in the officer corps and, even more, to restructure the process of military decision making, elevating some groups in the military hierarchy and demoting others. Most important, they have the duty to insist that military capabilities be consistent with political objectives. Nevertheless, civilian control and national security are badly served if civilians do not simultaneously recognize the importance of vesting responsibility and authority for certain matters in the officer corps — if, even while reforming, they do not recognize that there are some matters that must be delegated to the military. Civilians must know not only how to direct but also how to delegate, rendering "unto the civilians the things that are civilian, and unto the brass the things that are brass."[3] A failure to respect this basic principle of military policy will yield not coherence but institutional confusion and strategic disarray.

American defense policy has reached a critical turning point. The defense buildup engineered by the Reagan administration has now run its course; public support for defense spending has eroded. The nation has begun to turn its attention to the far-reaching problems revealed in the two great deficits in our national economic accounts: the extraordinary gap between expenses and revenues and that between exports and imports. Renewed attention is being given to the disproportionate burden the United States carries as the leader of the Western Alliance. Defense spending, having increased substantially in the first half of the 1980s — the third such period of prolonged growth in the postwar era — now seems likely to remain flat in real terms for the remainder of the 1980s and into the 1990s. Quite possibly it may decline.

The prospective reduction in military spending makes imperative a redirection of American defense strategy. Above all, it requires pruning the lush growth of strategic concepts that arose in the 1980s to justify the Reagan defense program. The new direction that should be taken, and the corresponding changes in strategic nuclear and general-purpose forces that are required, I have treated at length in a companion volume entitled *The Future of American Strategy*. The skeptical eye cast on "military reform" in the following pages should not be taken to reflect a numbing complacency about the status quo, for the reformation of American strategy — with all this implies for force disposition, weapons deployment, and spending levels — is indeed a necessity. It would be redundant, in the present work, to spell out in detail the strategic changes I believe are most desirable. Still, the political and strategic implications of U.S. military capabilities cannot be entirely neglected here. Defense policy inescapably raises the question of the relationship between political interest and military power, and without a clear view of what those interests are and what that relationship should be, the effort to transform the military establishment is not likely to yield a profitable result. "War cannot be divorced from political life," as Carl von Clausewitz observed, "and whenever this occurs in our thinking about war, the many links that connect the two elements are destroyed and we are left with something pointless and devoid of sense."[4]

The contemporary movement for military reform has often forgotten this admonition. There is, as we shall see, a curious disjunction within the reform movement. On questions of high policy or grand strategy, the reformers are all over the map — some are interventionists and others noninterventionists, some wish to begin withdrawing American ground forces from Central Europe, others seek to strengthen that commitment. Only on questions directly relating to the military's professional function is there a consensus among the reformers, but it is a consensus divorced from political considerations. This is in itself a serious error; but it has also led to a species of double-talk that does no service to the debate over American military policy. When some reformers celebrate the advantages of maneuver warfare for ground forces while simultaneously adopting a noninterventionary stance toward non-European contingencies and urging the withdrawal of American ground forces from Europe, one is left wondering on what terrain these forces would maneuver. In this instance, as in others, the strategic and operational critiques have proceeded on two different tracks, and the result has often been a curious mixture of false promise and internal inconsistency.

The consequences of this divorce between military capability and political object will be explored further in part 2 of this work, and there I will attempt to show why the military capabilities much criticized by the reformers — the heavy Army divisions capable of intensive operations in the first stages of a European war, the Navy's large-deck aircraft carriers, the Air Force's long-range bombers — do represent wise choices from the standpoint of political and strategic desirability. In part 1, I assess main conundrums of American civil-military relations and attempt to sort out the proper division of responsibility among the civilian and military institutions competing for the authority and power to determine military policy. In the aftermath of this examination it will be possible to assess the main challenge raised by the military reformers —a challenge directed against the competence of the existing set of military professionals and one that raises profound institutional questions. That initial inquiry, in turn, will allow us to see in what areas further institutional reforms are desirable, and where they are not.

I · AMERICAN CIVIL-MILITARY RELATIONS IN THEORY AND PRACTICE

1 · The Division of Responsibility

STRATEGY, OPERATIONS, AND ADMINISTRATION

The principle that ought to guide us in determining the appropriate division of authority between civilians and the military is suggested by Clausewitz's famous observation that war "has its own grammar, but not its own logic." Neither war nor preparation for war is an enterprise undertaken for itself. "Being incomplete and self-contradictory, it cannot follow its own laws, but has to be treated as a part of some other whole; the name of which is policy." Its conduct must consequently be subject to the direction of the statesman. For Clausewitz, as for us, the dictum that war is an instrument of policy was a justification of civilian control of the military: "The assertion that a major military development, or the plan for one, should be a matter for *purely military* opinion is unacceptable and can be damaging. It is in any case a matter of common experience that despite the great variety and development of modern war its major lines are still laid down by governments: in other words, if we are to be technical about it, by a purely political and not a military body. This is as it should be." Clausewitz also recognized, however, that there were some stages in the study of warfare where such a point of view "would not have been much help and might have been distracting." Policy, he noted, "will not extend its influence to operational details. Political considerations do not determine the posting of guards or the employment of patrols."[1] Some spheres of military activity involved purely military considerations and required evaluation from a military standpoint. All operations that exerted influence on the ends for which the war was being conducted, however, required the direction of policy. This concept of the "dual nature of war," Samuel P. Huntington has written, is the basic element in Clausewitz's theory of warfare: "War is at one and the same time an autonomous science with its own method and goals and yet a subordinate science in that its ultimate purposes come from outside itself. This concept of war is a true professional one, embodying as it does the essentials of any profession: the delimitation of a unique subject matter independent of other human thought and activity and the recognition of the limits of this subject matter within the total framework of human activity and purpose."2

Harmonizing political ends with military means is no easy task, and there is a sense in which the problem was greatly complicated by the emergence of professional military institutions in the nineteenth century. The great commanders of the preceding epoch, Frederick II of Prussia and Napoleon I of France, were also heads of state, a combination that often gave them decisive advantages over their opponents. With the separation of political and military function that accompanied the rise of military professionalism in the nineteenth century there also arose the problem of coordinating the two, and indeed the great conflicts of the twentieth century witnessed sharp conflict between statesmen and soldiers over the proper boundaries of their respective responsibilities. The acknowledgment of civilian supremacy over strategy, at least in the United States, was a long time in coming, a point revealed in the dispute between Truman and MacArthur over the conduct of the Korean War, in which MacArthur claimed an autonomy and a strategic aim that were wholly inconsistent with the evolving limited-war strategy of the Democrats (and that also, as it happened, were looked upon with disfavor by the Joint Chiefs of Staff, then headed by General Omar Bradley). Even in the late 1950s and early 1960s, Air Force generals and Navy admirals took a view of their responsibilities in the articulation of nuclear strategy that is now acknowledged to lie in the province of the statesman.3

Those concerned with establishing civilian supremacy in strategy in the United States often read back into the past the conflicts of their own time, seeing a division between civil and military authorities in the conduct of the two world wars that was in reality of a different character from what they assumed.4 The view that saw Germany's war plan in 1914 as something foisted upon civilian authorities by the military is perhaps the most striking instance of this phenomenon. In retrospect, to be sure, it is astonishing that the political authorities viewed war planning as something entirely within the province of the military, as if it were no concern to them whether Germany had more than one war plan (which it did not) or whether German armies marched through Belgium in the attempt to defeat France. Still, it is doubtful that intensive consultation between political and military authorities would have altered the basic complexion of the Schlieffen Plan. In the end, it was not the preeminence of the "cult of the offensive" in Germany but the logic of the prewar alliance system and the political ambitions of the antagonists that converted a local war in the Balkans into World War I. In attacking France, Germany correctly anticipated that France would come to the aid of her Russian ally and launch an offensive aimed at the recovery of Alsace-Lorraine; and when it became clear that the violation of Belgian neutrality might bring Great Britain into the war, German civil authorities consoled themselves with the thought that it would all be over by Christmas — that is, before British sea power could be brought into play. They took no account of the British Expeditionary Force, which played such a critical role in forcing a German retreat at the Battle of the Marne. This political calculation, in turn, underlined the need for rapid victory against France that would free up resources for combat against Russia. The military capabilities of the Russians were greatly exaggerated by Germany, as the extraordinary German victories at Tannenberg and the Masurian Lakes showed, but that is something that could not have been known at the time. Had the German General Staff not devised the Schlieffen Plan, therefore, it would have been necessary for civilians to invent it. As Paul Kennedy has rightly said, "There were no defensive strategies, because they were not wanted; there were no alternatives, because inflexibility was as much in the mind as it was in the railway timetable; there were no schemes for stalemate and compromise, because a swift and absolute victory was what was demanded; and there was little civilian control over the military because very often they both had the same objectives and shared a common ideology."[5]

If the outbreak of war in 1914 does not show a radical dissimilarity in perspective among civilians and the military, it does attest to the difficulty of harmonizing political ends and military means and the consequent necessity of clear civilian direction. Perhaps the most famous instance of this difficulty was the conjunction in France during the interwar period of a defensive military strategy based on the Maginot Line, with a set of diplomatic commitments in Eastern Europe that required France to take offensive action in the event of a German move to the east.[6] Another is the American naval bill of 1916, which called for massive building of battleships and armored cruisers. When the United States intervened in the European war the following year, it became apparent that the naval building program was focused on the wrong class of ships. The Allied powers were in no need of additional battleships, but there was a pressing need for large numbers of destroyers to combat the German submarine menace — something that could have been anticipated the previous year had an attempt been made to coordinate the American naval building program with policy.[7]

Nor has the challenge of harmonizing political ends with military means lost its salience in the nuclear age. The nuclear revolution has not invalidated Clausewitz's dictum, but it has affected the division of civil-military responsibility in two vital respects. In the first place, it has long been apparent that *any* use of nuclear weapons would raise political and strategic issues of the most profound character. In the nuclear age, civilians therefore have operational responsibilities that in an earlier time would have been appropriately assigned to the military, and they must play the key role in elaborating deterrent strategies. In the second place, the proper development of strategic weapons requires scientific expertise of a very high order — some of which, but by no means all, can be lodged in the military services. In the nuclear age, statesmen are therefore forced to make the strategic judgment as to what is desirable and the scientific judgment — on the basis of the best scientific and military advice they can receive — as to what is possible. Both these considerations are displayed in the contemporary debate over the wisdom and possibility of constructing ballistic missile defenses, a debate whose resolution is wholly a civilian responsibility. "We may as well admit," wrote Bernard Brodie in his *Strategy in the Missile Age*, "that the strictly tactical problem of destroying Manhattan is already absurdly easy." Time, Brodie thought, "promises to make it no less easy. That is only to say that its protection, if it can be protected, is henceforward a strategic and political problem rather than a tactical one."[8] It was also therefore a problem for civilian, not military resolution.

This conception of the relationship between civilian and military spheres of competence and their corresponding spheres of decision is relevant to all issues governing the use of force. Yet there is a vast range of other activities necessary for the successful functioning of a military organization to which this functional division does not apply. In both war and peace, soldiers must be fed and clothed, they must be provided with weapons and ammunition, the sick and wounded among them must be cared for. In supplying the vast wants of a military organization, an equally vast range of skills is required, skills entirely different from those acquired from the study of military science. As Alfred Thayer Mahan wrote in his valuable treatise on this subject, the activities connected with naval administration "differ from those common to civil life only in a certain particularity of method. This is true in principal measure of the financial management, of the medical establishment, and to a considerable though much smaller degree of the manufacturing processes connected with the production of naval material." Because of the vast array of nonmilitary skills required to produce all the goods and services needed for successful military operations, it might seem to follow that we should want a businessman in charge of supplying those wants as efficiently as possible. For Mahan, however, this was not the case: "It by no means follows that those departments would be better administered under men of civil habits of thought than by those of military training. The method exists for the result, and an efficient fighting body is not to be attained by weakening the appreciation of military necessities at the very fountain head of their supply in the administration."[9]

The recognition of the importance of such administrative skills in satisfying the wants of military organizations has led many presidents to believe that the first prerequisite for a competent Secretary of Defense is experience as a successful businessman. Charles E. Wilson (General Motors), Neil H. McElroy (Procter and Gamble), and Robert McNamara (Ford) all had this as their primary qualification. Wilson's view was summed up in his remark that he would "'leave the military stuff up to the military' and take charge of what he called 'production'; he would 'manage' not 'make' military policy." McElroy's tenure as Secretary of Defense was shorter and more difficult: "He arrived at the Pentagon with Sputnik and remained in orbit thereafter."[10] His resignation in 1958 represented the end of a certain kind of Secretary of Defense. Critics wondered why a man whose only prior experience had been marketing soap should be charged with supervising the military establishment, and it was no doubt with him primarily in mind that Bernard Brodie wrote in 1959 that "the secretaries of Defense and of the three services usually tend toward a narrow view of their administrative function, and incline to avoid if they can intervention in what they call 'strictly military decisions,' though they are not always permitted to. Since they are normally selected for talents in fields other than the military and rarely tarry long in their high public posts, their modesty is probably for the best."[11]

Eisenhower's last Secretary of Defense, Thomas Gates, and then Robert McNamara under the Democrats, represented a sharp, and enduring, change from the prevailing pattern, for both took seriously their responsibilities for strategy. McNamara, to be sure, touched everything, and indeed he made a number of changes in the administration of the Pentagon consistent with the prior conception of the office of the Secretary of Defense. He insisted that civilians do a better job in estimating the overall costs of military programs and therefore required that the defense budget be calculated each year on a moving five-year plan. He consolidated a number of functions that had previously been performed separately by each of the services through his creation of defensewide agencies responsible for mapping, intelligence, and many minor procurement functions. And with less success, he instituted policies of "total package procurement" designed to improve the acquisition of weapons systems — though as it happened the cost overruns on military systems that occurred in the 1960s represented no real improvement over the previous decade.[12] Still, his reign at the Pentagon was the most significant of all, and it is impossible to form an assessment of American civil-military relations without continual reference to his achievements — and failures.

Perhaps the most mature expression of the administrative conception of civilian responsibilities came from Under Secretary David Packard, who instituted major reforms of the weapons acquisition process while his superior, Melvin Laird, was preoccupied with effecting the disengagement of American ground forces from Vietnam. The fundamental intent of the Packard initiatives was to structure the process of decision making so as to ensure that considerations of efficiency were fully taken into account in the development of new weapons. He established a group within the Office of the Secretary of Defense responsible for providing an independent source of cost estimates, and he insisted that cost be one of the primary objectives in the design of new weapons. He also sought to encourage competition among contractors through competitive fly-offs. The initiatives, it is true, were not purely administrative. The injunction to "design to cost" reflected in part the judgment, preeminently military, that the services had unwisely sacrificed quantity to quality in developing new weapons. On the whole, however, the initiatives reflected a sound appraisal of the respective responsibilities of the military and civilians in military administration. Military effectiveness, determined by the professional military, remained the ultimate criterion. Decision making was structured, however, to ensure that cost was taken into account throughout, an injunction that in turn reflected two strategic judgments: first, that funds for defense were likely to be curtailed in coming years, and second, that the business of fielding new weaponry was not so urgent from a strategic point of view that an ordered process of development would have to be sacrificed, thus entailing the dangers of concurrent development and production that had been amply demonstrated in the 1950s and 1960s.*

---

*On the Packard reforms, see Dews et al., *Acquisition Policy Effectiveness*, p. 2. Many of the administrative changes called for by the President's Blue Ribbon Commission on Defense Management in 1986, chaired by Packard, represented a return to the practices that Packard had pioneered as Under Secretary of Defense during the first Nixon administration. Among other things, the commission called for less emphasis on rigid military specifications, a higher priority to building and testing prototypes before proceeding with full-scale development, greater emphasis on operational testing, im-

In strategy, operations, and administration, then, there ought to be a division of function between civilians and the military corresponding to their capabilities and responsibilities. Yet the relationship that exists in one sphere should be the opposite of that in the other. So far as operations are concerned, military organizations represent means to a strategic end that ought to be determined by civilians. "War in general, and the commander in any specific instance, is entitled to require that the trend and designs of policy shall not be inconsistent with these means. That, of course, is no small demand; but however much it may affect political aims in a given case, it will never do more than modify them. The political object is the goal, war is the means of reaching it, and means can never be considered in isolation from their purpose."[13] For administration the same proviso applies. The end is to produce an instrument of war, and all skills necessary to attain this result ought to be subordinate to that end. However considerations of efficiency may affect this end in a given case, they will never do more than modify it.[14] The wants of an army and a navy must be satisfied, of course, as efficiently as possible. But the method exists for the result. If strategy is thus the "art of distributing and applying military means to fulfill the ends of policy,"[15] military administration is the art of managing a diverse array of activities essentially civil to fulfill the ends of war.

THE FOUNDATION OF AMERICAN MILITARY PROFESSIONALISM: ROOT AND MAHAN

The debate that arose about the turn of the century over the creation of a Chief of Staff for the Army and a Chief of Naval Operations for the Navy illustrates these questions in some detail, for it revolved around the problem of assigning to civilians and the military their appropriate roles in determining strategy, operations, and administration. For both

---

proved incentives for program managers, and a reduction of red tape. As the commission argued: "Short, unambiguous lines of communication among levels of management, small staffs of highly competent professional personnel, an emphasis on innovation and productivity, smart buying practices, and, most importantly, a stable environment of planning and funding — all are characteristic of efficient and successful management. These characteristics should be hallmarks of defense acquisition. They are, unfortunately, antithetical to the process the Congress and the Department of Defense have created to conduct much of defense acquisition over the years." President's Blue Ribbon Commission on Defense Management, *An Interim Report to the President* (Washington, D.C., 28 February 1986), p. 13. See also the commission's full report, *A Quest for Excellence: Final Report to the President by the President's Blue Ribbon Commission on Defense Management* (Washington, D.C., 1986).

services, the difficulty was to establish an organizational relationship among civilians and the military that would reflect the special expertise and responsibility of both. It was then as now much easier, however, to prescribe an appropriate relationship in theory than to realize it in practice. In practice there were continual debates as to the level of military professionalism — that is, the relation of operational and strategic questions to the problems of high policy — and the scope of military professionals — that is, the relation between civilians and the military in the sphere of administration.[16]

The two men most responsible for bringing reform to the Army and the Navy were, respectively, Elihu Root and Alfred Thayer Mahan. As Paul Hammond summarized their accomplishments in his classic study of the American defense establishment in the twentieth century: Mahan "rescued the Navy, and Root, the Army, from their technicism. Each gave his service a central rationale for its purpose as a whole, though what each gave was quite different: Mahan provided the Navy with a strategy; Root, the Army with an organization."[17]

During Mahan's years in the service, the Navy Department was headed by a civilian secretary, but the real locus of control lay in the hands of bureau chiefs responsible for "the movement of ships, the recruitment and assignment of personnel, the construction and repair of ships, and the procurement of supplies and equipment."[18] The bureau chiefs were authorized to act in the name of the Secretary of the Navy, and each enjoyed powerful connections in Congress. There was consequently very little central direction. Two great faults came to be identified with these arrangements: First, there was nobody to coordinate the work of the bureaus in naval administration, and hence the business of naval administration was insufficiently subordinate to the criterion of military effectiveness. Second, there was no professional man in charge of the preparation of war plans and of coordinating the movements of the fleet in war. Mahan was concerned particularly with the latter problem, whereas a group that came to be known as the radical reformers was concerned with both.

There is no mystery about why Mahan believed the Navy required an office staffed by professional line officers responsible for directing the fleet in war and preparing naval strategy. The principles of strategy, for Mahan, were unchanging. In naval warfare, command of the sea required the destruction of the enemy battle fleet, which in turn required the concentration of one's own. Naval professionalism thus consisted in the first place of understanding naval strategy; the highest skill of the naval officer was directing the fleet in war. Curiously enough, however,

Mahan did not believe that the Chief of Naval Operations (CNO), as this professional naval man came to be called, should direct the work of the bureaus. This responsibility Mahan allocated to the civilian Secretary of the Navy. His failure to do so is curious precisely because his conception of naval administration, noted earlier, seemed to call for a man with an acute appreciation of military necessities at the "fountain head of their supply in the administration." It was on just this point, moreover, that a group of insurgent officers — of whom perhaps the most representative figure was William S. Sims — came to differ with Mahan. The radical reformers insisted upon the need for professional direction of the entire naval establishment. Without such professional control, they believed, it would be impossible to coordinate the work of the bureaus. The evil consequences to which such absence of central direction had led in the design of warships constituted the central indictment the radical reformers brought against the existing bureau system, but centralization under a civilian secretary could not remedy these evils, they believed, since the secretary lacked the technical competence to adjudicate competing bureau claims.

There was a potential challenge to civilian control in the conceptions of the office of CNO advanced by both Mahan and the insurgents. The danger posed by the latter was well understood by most Secretaries of the Navy. Indeed, the Secretary of the Navy during whose tenure the office of Chief of Naval Operations was established, Josephus Daniels (1913–20), was particularly insistent on limiting the scope of the CNO's powers. But there was an equal danger to civilian control in Mahan's concept of the office. To commit oneself to his conception of naval operations, with its emphasis on concentrated naval forces capable of distant operations, carried with it a host of political implications, particularly toward commerce and colonies; and it was not within the province of the military to determine whether the United States was to become an imperial power in the Pacific. The acquisition of the Philippines owed something to Mahan's influence, for the war plan that sent Admiral Dewey into Manila Bay during the 1898 war with Spain had itself been devised by a naval officer of low rank under the influence of Mahan's precepts. This maneuver, however, had far-reaching consequences: once the military was in possession of the Philippines it proved impossible to leave, and thus the United States came to hold a piece of territory that immensely complicated the strategic equation in the western Pacific for the next four decades.[19] It is equally true, however, that the failure to establish an office with control over both operations and administration would leave civilians with responsibilities they were not professionally equipped to execute. That failure, in turn, might prove even more dangerous than the military challenge to civilian control.

The reforms that Elihu Root brought to the War Department raised a similar set of issues. The "real object of having an army," Root announced in one of the capable reports he prepared as Secretary of War, "is to provide for war." In making such provision during the Spanish-American War, however, the Army had shown itself sadly deficient. To remedy this deficiency Root proposed creating a General Staff that would function as the "brain of the army." He illustrated the duties of such a body of officers "by taking for example an invasion of Cuba, such as we were all thinking about a few years ago."

> It is easy for a President, or a general acting under his direction, to order that 50,000 or 100,000 men proceed to Cuba and capture Havana. To make an order which has any reasonable chance of being executed he must do a great deal more than that. He must determine how many men shall be sent and how they shall be divided among the different arms of the service, and how they shall be armed, and equipped; and to do that he must get all the information possible about the defenses of the place to be captured and the strength and character and armament of the forces to be met. He must determine at what points and by what routes the place shall be approached, and at what point his troops shall land in Cuba; and for this purpose he must be informed about the various harbors of the island and the depth of their channels; what classes of vessels can enter them; what the facilities for landing are; how they are defended; the character of the roads leading from them to the place to be attacked; the character of the intervening country; how far it is healthful or unhealthful; what the climate is liable to be at the season of the proposed movement; the temper and sympathies of the inhabitants; the quantity and kind of supplies that can be obtained from the country; the extent to which transportation can be obtained, and a great variety of other things which will go to determine whether it is better to make the approach from one point or from another, and to determine what it will be necessary for the army to carry with it in order to succeed in moving and living and fighting.[20]

This advice was unexceptionable as far as it went, but it still left the General Staff, once it was created, in a quandary as to precisely what it was supposed to do. For what operations should the American Army plan? In the coming years it would receive very little political guidance about the occasions on which and the areas in which it might be employed. Its difficulties in this regard, and the sensitivities it might arouse were it to fulfill such duties faithfully, are well illustrated by the reaction of Woodrow Wilson — "trembling and white with passion" — on learning the news that "the General Staff was preparing plans for the eventuality of war with Germany." Wilson ordered an investigation into the truth of the story. If it were true, every officer on the General Staff, he told an associate, was to be relieved.[21]

The diplomacy of isolation and the traditional American suspicion of things military thus did not foster a climate conducive to realistic planning, even at a time — perhaps especially at a time, like the autumn of 1915 — when involvement in war became something more than an unthinkable possibility. There was nevertheless a great deal of work to be done at the turn of the century to prepare the Army for virtually any war it might become engaged in. The strength of the Army was scattered about in dozens of posts on the western plains, deployed for an era that was past and prepared to fight a people whose strength was now completely broken. The strategic role Root had foreseen for the Army — which centered on the conquest of the Philippines and Cuba — was gradually repudiated as public opinion turned against imperialism. But the Army's new organization remained. Subsequent Chiefs of Staff were thus led away from the planning of operations and into the Army's administration. This conception of the office of Chief of Staff, quite different from the one Root had initially envisaged for it, yet a logical implication of its existence, inevitably brought the Chief of Staff into conflict with the interlocking set of congressional and Army bureau interests then in control of the Army's administration.[22]

The primacy of the Chief of Staff over all elements of the Army was not finally established until World War II, when the office came into the hands of George C. Marshall. What is of interest to us is not the events behind the establishment of this primacy but rather the logic that underlay it and the view of professionalism it advanced. By contrast with the moderate reformers of the Navy, the Army's concept of its professionalism had both a lower level and a wider scope. Its role in operations did not lead inexorably, as it had in the hands of Mahan, to a particular conception of national strategy. Throughout this period, the Army lacked the strategic vision that was an essential part of the Navy's reason for existence. The Chief of Staff, on the other hand, was led to assert a far-reaching control over the administration of the Army, for the most part with the blessing of the Secretary of War, whereas most Secretaries of the Navy stoutly resisted such forays of professional Navy men into the overall control of administration.

The experience of both the Army and Navy in the United States appears to indicate that we are in the presence of a problem of government organization to which there is no perfect solution. Because civilians and the military alike have appropriate roles in both strategy and administration, it is very difficult to specify the formal relationship that ought to exist between them. To place a general staff over the whole of the military, responsible for both operational planning and all the activities associated with administration, raises the danger that civilian leaders will lose control of grand strategy and that the wants of the military will be inefficiently supplied. To place a civilian at the head of the administration, however, raises the possibility that the criterion of military effectiveness, by which the successful administration of a military establishment must principally be measured, will be lost sight of and "efficiency" for its own sake will gain an unhealthy and unnecessary predominance over the whole. And because civilian leaders are not professionally equipped to plan and direct military operations; the absence of a staff to serve as the "brain" of an armed service will make it very difficult for the military to fulfill any strategic role at all, much less one devised by itself.

The Military Professional, Fusionism, and the Bureaucratic Revisionists

The theory of civil-military relations advanced here is quite similar in spirit to that set forth a generation ago by Samuel P. Huntington in his classic work *The Soldier and the State*. In that work Huntington distinguished between "objective" and "subjective" civilian control, seeking to vindicate the one and condemn the other. "Civilian control in the objective sense," he wrote, "is the maximizing of military professionalism. More precisely, it is that distribution of political power between military and civilian groups which is most conducive to the emergence of professional attitudes and behavior among the members of the officer corps." Objective and subjective civilian control, Huntington argued, are directly opposed: "The essence of objective civilian control is the recognition of autonomous military professionalism; the essence of subjective civilian control is the denial of an independent military sphere."

Both systems of civilian control seek to minimize military power: "Objective civilian control achieves this reduction by professionalizing the military, by rendering them politically sterile and neutral. At the same time, it preserves that essential element of power which is necessary for the existence of a military profession." Whereas objective civilian control seeks to militarize the military and make them the tool of the state, subjective civilian control "achieves its ends by civilianizing the military, making them the mirror of the state." The defect of subjective civilian control, in Huntington's view, was that it was inconsistent with the protection of national security, which required the development and maintenance of a professional corps with an expert understanding of the nature of contemporary warfare. War, on this view, was too specialized a business to be left to civilians. "Subjective civilian control is fundamentally out of place in any society in which the division of labor has been carried to the point where there emerges a distinct class of specialists in the management of violence."[23]

The assumptions underlying Huntington's theory of objective civilian control are the same as those governing the traditional model of administration (not to be confused with the related, yet distinct, idea of business administration considered earlier). "Traditional administrative theory," as Richard Betts had observed, "posits a dichotomy between politics and administration: elected leaders and political appointees establish policy; politically neutral career bureaucrats execute the politicians' decisions."[24] Politics is the realm of ends, values, and choice; administration that of means, facts, and expertise. On this view the discretion exercised by the civil administrator or military professional is more apparent than real, and the tension between democratic precept and professional elite dissolves. "The policy to be set is simply a function of the goal to be achieved and the state of the world."[25] Comparable assumptions underlie the traditional conception of the judge as a neutral official who applies settled, general rules to particular facts.

Just as there is a basic similarity in the assumptions underlying the ideas of objective civilian control, traditional administrative theory, and judicial review, so too the critiques of each idea follow a remarkably similar line of attack. In each case the critics—"fusionists," "bureaucratic revisionists," and "legal realists," respectively—argue that the discretion exercised by military professionals, civil administrators, and judges is far wider than the traditional model assumes.[26] Partly this is because the general directives that the technical experts are required to implement are vague or ambiguous. The Supreme Court, as Justice Felix Frankfurter once put it, "is compelled to put meaning into the Constitution not to take it out."[27] Statements of security policy by civilian leaders tend to be equally vague or abstract; invariably they fail to include criteria for ranking values against one another, which is indispensable to allocating resources if budgets are limited (as they always are). Subordinate organizations tend to acquire an intellectual outlook and bureaucratic interests of their own: it was a familiar observation (before deregulation changed the character of the political landscape) that administrative agencies like the ICC, the FTC, and the CAB often served the interests of those they were ostensibly regulating; equally familiar is the complaint that the military services have a set of "wish lists" that correspond to internal organizational or bureaucratic imperatives bearing little relation to military necessity.

Perhaps of greatest importance is that, in all these fields, the distinction between functions based on ends and means, though easy to make in theory, is highly problematic in practice. The institutional arrangement that corresponds to this functional differentiation is extremely difficult to specify, because in practice a decision based on "military effectiveness" will have implications for administrator and strategist alike. The design of a tank, if too complicated and costly, will affect how many can be procured — which in turn may determine the possibilities of single- or dual-source procurement, a matter that ought to be resolved by the specialist in business administration. The weight of such a tank, in turn, will affect its suitability for rapid deployment, the capabilities for which ought to be determined by the statesman on the basis of his overall grand strategy. The intrinsic trade-off between strategic and tactical mobility thus touches more than one area of responsibility. The protection afforded by heavier armor may dramatically increase tactical mobility on the battlefield, but the additional weight will probably make deployment to a theater of operations less rapid. What seems at first to be a relatively straightforward military issue — the design of the proverbial "best tank" — in fact raises a host of administrative and political questions, the decisions on which constitute a kind of seamless web.

The fluidity of strategic, military, and administrative considerations does not invalidate the theory of civil-military relations advanced by Huntington, though it is often taken to do so. The most explicit repudiation of "objective civilian control" was made by the "fusionists," who denied the possibility of functional specialization and argued that it had "become impossible to maintain the distinction between political and military functions at the highest level of government."[28] The fluidity of these categories, however, does not mean that the distinction between statesmen and soldiers and that between soldiers and administrators are without value. On the contrary, it merely indicates that the work of one group may easily obstruct the work of the other. Consequently an appropriate pattern of civil-military relations requires that each group display a certain deference toward the other's special expertise and responsibility. The military is required to understand that the use of force — and indeed the whole panoply of peacetime preparation to that end — is a deeply political issue and that the autonomy of military organizations is impossible to justify if it is not in harmony with the strategic outlook of the nation's civilian leaders. The civilians, on the other hand, must understand that there are certain kinds of decisions that the military is specially competent to make. Civilian leadership must know, therefore, not only how to decide but also how to delegate.

None of this means that Huntington's conception of civil-military relations is without defects. Arguably, he located military professionalism at too high a level and gave it too narrow a scope. "Strategic planning," Huntington has written elsewhere, involves such matters as "the assessment of threats and needs, and then the determination of priorities among regions (e.g. Europe versus the Persian Gulf), types of forces (e.g. nuclear versus conventional, regular vs. reserves), force dispositions (e.g. forward deployments versus enhanced mobility), timing requirements (e.g. modernization versus readiness), and weapons (e.g. smaller numbers of highly sophisticated weapons versus larger numbers of less capable weapons)." Military officers, he insisted, "should play a central role in the development of overall strategic plans."[29] Yet such a conception of military professionalism raises the authority of the military to a level its professional expertise does not and cannot justify, even with substantial political guidance. The allocation of resources among regions, as well as force dispositions, depends upon an assessment of *interest*, the choice between a nuclear and a conventional emphasis in strategy rests upon an assessment of the *risk* one is willing to incur, and the choice between modernization and readiness depends ultimately upon an assessment of the *likelihood of war* within the near future. All these matters require political understanding and political judgment. Only the quantity-quality trade-off raises primarily military issues, and even this matter rests upon a prior determination of manpower policy (a draft or volunteer force) that is also clearly within the jurisdiction of civilians. Nor is this all. Primarily political questions are also raised by "the whole series of closely related issues as to the circumstances under which and how American forces would be used in combat: for example, offensively or defensively, in long wars or short wars, unilaterally or in conjunction with allies, in gradual increments or in a massive initial commitment." It was Robert McNamara's great accomplishment as Secretary of Defense to insist upon the right of civilians to make such determinations. It is true that he went too far in this respect, often meddling in operational details and sometimes (wrongly) acting as if the distinctive expertise that lay at the heart of the military's claim to professionalism were nonexistent. Nevertheless, the assertion of civilian supremacy in strategy was entirely justified.

Huntington also provided the military with too narrow a scope. Although in theory it seems to make sense to restrict the military to authority over military affairs, in practice it is frequently necessary to place under military command activities that, in Mahan's phrase, "differ from those common to civil life only in a certain particularity of method." This is so for two reasons: because the military is less likely than are experts in business administration to sacrifice military effectiveness to administrative efficiency, and because it is usually desirable for organizational reasons to vest responsibility for particular tasks in a single office. This was one of the central insights of David Packard in his reform program at the outset of the 1970s. One of the most important aspects of the Packard reforms was strengthening the authority of the military officers who managed weapons-procurement programs. In part Packard sought to do this by giving them a clear written charter and by lengthening their job tenure. But he also recognized that their business skills were often deficient and therefore established military training courses and schools to prepare them for the job.[30] This had the liability from the standpoint of civil-military relations of deflecting these officers from their primarily military orientation (a point emphasized by the military reformers), yet there was little alternative to doing so. Placing civilians in the position of program managers would have incurred the opposite liability, and dividing the position between a civilian and a military man would have sacrificed the organizational virtue of concentrating responsibility for particular programs in a single head.

The fluidity and interpenetration of strategic, operational, and administrative questions makes it very difficult, in the end, to specify the exact level and scope of military authority, and we ought not to fall victim to the error of treating the subject with more precision than the material will bear. Indeed, Huntington's theory of civil-military relations is perhaps most vulnerable on precisely these grounds. In *The Soldier and the State* he placed insufficient emphasis on the *ethic* that ought to govern the relationship between civilians and the military and showed excessive faith in the formal institutional arrangements governing civil-military relations. Perhaps the most striking example of this tendency is his argument that the competing pretensions of civilian and military authority were best satisfied by a "balanced" type of executive civil-military relations, one that "assigns to the President a purely political function: the decision of the highest policy issues and the general supervision of the military establishment. Beneath him is the secretary, also a purely political figure, responsible for the entire military organization. Below the secretary, the hierarchy divides into military and administrative components." Contrasting this type of organization with "coordinate" and "vertical" schemes, Huntington argued that "the balanced type of organization tends to maximize military professionalism and civilian control. Civilian and military responsibilities are clearly distinguished, and the latter are subordinated to the former. The President and the secretary handle political matters; the military chief military matters; and the staff or bureau chiefs administrative matters." This view, in turn, led Huntington to condemn the kind of relationship that existed among civilians and the military in the United States during World War II and to approve of the balanced organization that governed civil-military relations in Great Britain during World War I.[31]

Yet the condemnation of the one and the approval of the other are not warranted. In Britain civil-military relations during World War I followed a virtually pathological pattern, one perhaps most strikingly revealed in the bitter dispute between Douglas Haig and David Lloyd George over the appropriate strategy on the Western Front. Appalled by the huge number of men killed and wounded as a consequence of Haig's futile efforts to punch a hole in the German line, but too conscious of Haig's independent political standing to recall him, Lloyd George resorted to the dangerous expedient of lessening the number of men Haig had available on the Western Front so that the general could not attempt any more offensives. But this so stretched the line the British were attempting to maintain that it left the Allies dangerously vulnerable to the spring offensives undertaken in 1918 by Ludendorff. The episode is a classic instance of the danger that may arise when cooperation between civil and military authorities is absent.[32]

By contrast, American civil-military relations during World War II, though judged defective, were relatively harmonious and reasonably effective. The collaboration in administrative affairs between Chief of Staff George Marshall and Secretary of War Henry Stimson — each of whom had a well-founded regard for the other's integrity and competence — was quite successful. James Forrestal, first as Under Secretary and then as Secretary of the Navy, also devised a set of administrative controls that contributed much to the efficiency of the Navy Material Program and that also served to limit the pretensions of the Chief of Naval Operations, Admiral Ernest King.[33] And though the civilian secretaries were basically excluded from the most important deliberations on the strategy of the war, it is apparent that the key decisions were made by civilian leaders — that is, by Roosevelt in conjunction with other allied leaders and in consultation with the Combined Chiefs of Staff. The excessive influence of the military was felt not during but after the war, when the Army in particular was forced because of a continuing lack of civilian guidance to involve itself heavily in policy toward the occupation of former Axis territory.

An appropriate pattern of civil-military relations, then, depends not so much on the formal institutional arrangements among civilian and military leaders as on the attitude each adopts toward the other. The values Huntington sought to further in thus delimiting the appropriate level and scope of civilian and military authority are sensible ones, but beyond a certain point mere institutional arrangements cannot advance such values. They can be advanced, if at all, only by the mutual deference that has been the hallmark of all successful civil-military collaborations. Institutional arrangements, in this instance, cannot supply "by opposite and rival interests, the defect of better motives."[34] In this instance — as in others — there is no substitute for better motives.

2 · The Lack of Unified Direction

Every system of civil-military relations must contend with disputes over the level and scope of military authority, and finding the proper distribution of authority in the realms of strategy, operations, and administration is no easy thing. The task is complicated beyond all measure in the United States because of two additional factors that are in critical respects shared by no other major power. One is that in the United States civilian authority is divided between the executive and legislative branches of the national government; the other is that military expertise is divided among independent military services. Because civilian direction, when divided, is not authoritative, the military services are led to become involved in politics, seeking from one set of civilians what another would deny them. Because military expertise, when divided, is not authoritative, civilians are led to become involved in military matters. Whatever the inadequacies of "fusionism" in the realm of prescriptive or normative theory, at times it provides a striking description of the current condition of American civil-military relations, a state of affairs produced by powerful structural tendencies in our governing system.

The lack of unity on one side reinforces that on the other, and both phenomena acting together give our national security decision making its peculiar flavor, with implications that reach far beyond civil-military relations as such. The process of national security decision making in the United States tends to be at once more open and more resistant to change than that of other countries. When change occurs, it comes at the margin. Strategy tends to be pluralistic; military operations have been characterized by divided commands and discordant voices; and the administration of the services seems at times to resemble a commodities exchange, with procurement contracts bandied about like so many pork bellies, depending on the political power that can be brought to bear on their behalf. What Edmund Burke once said of the cabinet of Lord Chatham — it was, he thought, "an administration so checkered and speckled . . . a cabinet so variously inlaid . . . a piece of diversified mosaic . . . a tessellated pavement without cement"[1] — may justly be said of our system of defense decision making and our pattern of civil-military relations.

Congress and the Separation of Powers

In no other country is parliamentary involvement in national security affairs so great as in the United States. In the Congress there are four major committees (the Appropriations and Armed Services committees in each house) that review virtually the whole of the defense budget in a detailed manner, as well as a number of other committees (such as Government Operations) that wield significant power over parts of the Defense Department. Each of these committees has a distinct outlook and often has ties to different factions within the Pentagon. Each has shown an increasing propensity to make detailed changes in budgetary line items, which is perhaps the best indicator of increasing "micromanagement." Responding to the president's 1984 defense budget request, the House Armed Services Committee made adjustments to 424 out of 731 line items, the Senate committee to 450 out of 731; of the 1,129 line items in the DOD request to the appropriations committee, the House made adjustments in 766, the Senate in 710.[2]

Nor is the fractionalization of power confined to the legislative branch. In the gauntlet that is run by the military services in preparing a budget, a process nominally under the control of the Secretary of Defense, there are moments when the intervention of the National Security Council, the Office of Management and Budget, and the State Department may be decisive. Once in the Congress, the annual process starts at the beginning of the calendar year in January but recently has not ended until well after the beginning of the fiscal year in October — thus requiring the Department of Defense to operate on continuing resolutions. The multiplication of checks and balances in the defense decision making process is not conducive, to put it mildly, to what Alexander Hamilton called "energy" in governance. "Decision, activity, secrecy, and dispatch," he observed in his classic defense of the unity of the executive, "will generally characterize the proceedings of one man in a much more eminent degree than the proceedings of any greater number; and in proportion as the number is increased, these qualities will be diminished."[3]

Congressional involvement in national security affairs in general and in the defense budget in particular has grown sharply over the past two decades. There is no watershed in the supervision of the defense budget that has the same symbolic and practical import as the War Powers Act, but the increase in active involvement and "micromanagement" has all the same been relentless. Some of the most startling indexes of change are precisely quantifiable, such as

- the vast growth (from 114 in 1960 to 503 in 1984) in the total number of pages in the Appropriations Committee reports on the DOD budget, and an even larger increase for the authorizing committees (from 80 pages in 1965 to 858 in 1984);
- the sharp increase in the number of Pentagon reports mandated by Congress (from 36 in 1970 to 458 in 1984);
- the growth of supervisory power in the Armed Services committees, which authorized only a small portion of the defense budget in the early 1960s but which now authorize it entirely;
- and the increase in the number of staff, which has grown by about 400 percent since the 1960s.

The causes of the fractionalization of power are mainly constitutional. The Framers vested in Congress the power "to raise and support Armies" and "to provide and maintain a Navy"; they gave the president the office of commander-in-chief, thus allowing him to claim not merely "executive" powers but those that traditionally were the prerogative of the king. Competition between the two branches of government for control of the military is thus an inevitable feature of the American system of government; indeed, congressional deference toward the executive has been more the exception than the rule over the long history of American military policy. One need only think of the Committee on the Conduct of the War during the Civil War and the extensive power wielded by the chairmen of the congressional military committees from the end of the Civil War to the onset of World War II. Although the presidencies of Abraham Lincoln, Theodore Roosevelt, and Woodrow Wilson heralded the possibilities of presidential leadership, the more normal pattern from 1789 to 1945 was executive deference to the legislature. (There are few more pathetic spectacles in the history of American military policy than the way Congress mauled James Madison's polite requests for military preparations in the years before the War of 1812. Present difficulties pale by comparison.) Given the basic structure of our constitutional system, the power Congress currently enjoys is a more normal state of affairs than most critics (this one included) would care to admit. The reference point to which we instinctively recur — the postwar period of foreign policy consensus and congressional deference

— reflects the more abnormal pattern of presidential leadership and executive-congressional harmony.[4]

The vast increase in presidential power that marked the postwar period was largely the consequence of three novel factors: the experience of World War II, during which the scope of executive power was greatly enlarged; the repudiation of isolationism and the construction of a vast network of alliances and dependencies whose management, it was widely agreed, required the exercise of presidential power; and the peculiar psychological exigencies of the Cold War, whose effective conduct required Hamilton's executive qualities of "decision, activity, secrecy, and dispatch." The recent growth of congressional power over defense and foreign affairs, in turn, is largely a consequence of the two great failures of presidential power in the 1960s and 1970s: Vietnam put the presidency on the ropes; Watergate delivered the coup de grace. Part of the increase in congressional power might also plausibly be seen as a response to the assertion of executive power over the military in the 1960s under McNamara. In the 1950s, neither executive bureaucrats nor congressional staffers "micromanaged" the military services. The rise of the one was partly responsible for the increased interest of the other.

The consequences of civilian rivalry for control of military policy are mixed. The rivalry has the effect of maintaining a balance between the executive and legislative branches, as the Framers intended, and thus of guarding against a gradual concentration of power on either side. Congress certainly performed this checking role during the greater part of the Reagan administration, especially after the 1982 congressional elections changed its composition. The large number of adjustments to the defense budget requests submitted by Reagan in 1984 and subsequent years reflected not only "micromanagement" but also the belief that the Pentagon's budgetary requests were totally inconsistent with the need to reduce the budget deficit. Given the notorious gridlock that developed in the 1980s over the right way to achieve that objective — the president refusing to budge on taxes, the Congress unwilling to make further cuts in spending on entitlements — some form of "micromanagement" in defense was inevitable. There was no other way for Congress to express its dissatisfaction with the Reagan administration's priorities. The administration knew this. It understood that Congress would make cuts in its defense request. Its political calculation was that, given congressional sentiment, a higher defense request would in the end fare much better than a "realistic" one. And for this reason it is difficult to assign all the blame for the rise in congressional micromanagement to Congress alone. Part of the blame — perhaps the greater part — must fall on the administration itself.

The constant checking and division of power is the principal virtue of the American system of government, and that virtue was demonstrated anew in the 1980s by Congress's ability to check the excesses of the executive branch. But there can be too much of a good thing. The fractured character of the process is a nightmare from the standpoint of administrative efficiency. Across-the-board cuts in procurement contracts drive unit costs up substantially. With everything on the table until the last moment, defense contractors cannot make reliable plans, and the costs of their uncertainty are usually passed on to the taxpayer. The nature of the defense decision-making process, moreover, encourages bad habits on everybody's part. The military services believe that if they lose support for one weapons system in Congress they cannot apply the lost resources to other purposes, and hence they try to get everything they can while avoiding difficult choices and trade-offs themselves. The results of testing may kill a project in its early stages; mendacity can therefore be very rewarding. What a former British prime minister, Henry Asquith, once said of the War Office holds equally true for the contemporary American procurement commands: each has an incentive to keep three sets of figures — "one to mislead the public, another to mislead the Cabinet, and the third to mislead itself."[5]

The principal defect of the heightened congressional role is that it encourages the intrusion of narrow political considerations into the determination of matters that ought ideally to be resolved by professional experts. Institutionally Congress enjoys neither military nor administrative expertise. Individual members and standing committees, to be sure, have access to staff with genuine claims to such expertise; but the dominant consideration for congressmen is "the electoral connection."[6] To give Congress a major role in making military policy virtually ensures that considerations other than military effectiveness and administrative efficiency will continually affect the management of the military establishment. The most striking example of the intrusion of narrow political considerations into the defense budget is the support that liberal Democrats normally hostile to the Pentagon have given to weapons produced in their own states and districts: Alan Cranston's support of the B-1 bomber, the endorsement that Tip O'Neill, Robert Drinan, and Edward Kennedy gave to the F-18 (whose engine is produced in Massachusetts), the support of the New York delegation for the A-10 and the T-46 (both produced on Long Island) — all testify to the potency of electoral considerations. This propensity, however, is not confined to liberal Democrats. It occurs with the same frequency on both sides of the aisle.

These defects are inevitable to a certain degree, and as noted earlier, they are the mirror image of real virtues. However Congress is organized, its members will respond to the wishes of the voters in their own states and districts. The institution itself, moreover, has constitutional responsibilities that have almost always invited the close scrutiny (and consequent micromanagement) of the military. It is nevertheless true that some of the defects are magnified by two aspects of the current defense budget process that, at the same time, lack any real compensating virtues. One is the perpetuation of one-year budget plans as opposed to a two-year system. Another is the proliferation of committees in the Congress with supervision over the Defense Department. Each points to an area where reform is necessary.

SERVICISM AND THE MCNAMARA REVOLUTION

The relations that exist today among the military services and between the military services and civilian superiors are not the product of a single act. The most important milestones in the postwar period have been the 1947 National Security Act and the subsequent clarification of roles and missions among the services under the Truman administration (embodied in the 1948 Key West accord); the creation in 1958 of a set of unified commands with principal responsibility for the conduct of military operations within certain geographic areas, along with a number of specified commands under the control of the Air Force and responsible for airlift (MAC), strategic retaliation (SAC), and air defense (ADC); and the centralization of authority in the office of the Secretary of Defense carried out by Robert McNamara in the 1960s (the basis for which was laid in the 1949, 1953, and 1958 revisions to the 1947 National Security Act). Until the 1986 Goldwater-Nichols Act, there had been no extensive reorganizations at the Pentagon since the early 1960s, though the style of civilian leadership has varied extensively. Democratic administrations have sought to play a more active role in the management of military policy, while Republicans have generally been more willing to delegate certain decisions to each of the services. Yet there has never been widespread satisfaction with the pattern of civil-military relations these legislative acts and executive practices have yielded. Two problems persisted, each arising from the continuing existence of separate military departments: one is that operations tended to be characterized by multiple and conflicting counsels from each service; the second is that there was no source of dispassionate military advice on strategic planning and force development.[7]

It is not easy to assess the operational record of the American military since World War II. Douglas MacArthur's bold flanking move at Inchon is often held up by military reformers as the high point of postwar American operational art, after which there exists only a steady record of bungling and incompetence. The American combat record in Vietnam is, of course, exhibit A, but ample room is provided for lesser failures, from the abortive landing at the Bay of Pigs in 1961 to the costly attempt to recapture the *Mayaguez* in 1975, and from the humiliation at Desert One in 1980 to the destruction of the Marine compound in Beirut in 1983. These episodes reveal numerous mistakes in judgment, planning, and execution, and indeed in some cases they point to systemic flaws in higher defense organization. In each case, however, there were extenuating circumstances, and the impression we are often left with — that all would have gone well had our senior commanders not bungled the job — is more than a little unfair.

Perhaps the most striking feature of the postwar record is the relationship that exists between political failure and military incompetence.[8] When the political objectives set by civilian leaders were confused or wrongheaded, military operations usually fared no better. When those objectives were clear and attainable, the operational errors committed by the military were of little consequence. The liberation of Grenada has been condemned by critics on the usual grounds — interservice rivalry in the selection of the units committed to the invasion, poor intelligence, clumsy execution.[9] But these failures, such as they were, were entirely overshadowed by the fact that the objectives were realizable and were in fact achieved in short order. The attempt to rescue the American hostages in Iran in 1980 — the worst example on record of the deleterious effect of interservice rivalry on the conduct of operations — represented an act of total, though understandable, desperation. The odds against the successful execution of the mission as a whole were impossibly high, and even had things gone smoothly at Desert One, disasters probably awaited American commandos in the streets of Teheran.[10] In Beirut, the Marine commander failed to respond to the growing warning signs of terrorist attack on the Marine compound. Relevant intelligence was not passed down the chain of command, and the Army's offer of its counterterrorism experts was rebuffed.[11] But surely the larger failure lay in placing the Marines in Lebanon in the first place and then in failing to understand that the Israeli withdrawal from the mountains overlooking Beirut placed the American contingent in an untenable position and required its withdrawal.

The conduct of operations in Vietnam tells a similar tale. It is easy to dismiss Westmoreland's strategy in Vietnam as doomed to failure, not so easy to find an alternative that would have won the war. Some critics argue that Westmoreland's war of attrition was a waste of American energies and that a more successful strategy would have sought to isolate the South Vietnamese battlefield.[12] Others sharply criticize the lavish use of firepower in the Vietnamese countryside and call for a small unit war of posts.[13] But both lines of criticism — dissimilar though they are — contain serious flaws. "Isolating the battlefield" became a viable strategy only after the Tet offensive, which decimated the Viet Cong infrastructure in the South. By then the support of the American public for the war had collapsed. A war of posts, on the other hand, would have left American units exposed to piecemeal attacks, as Westmoreland feared. More important, successful counterinsurgency requires a strong political base, which could not be supplied by American troops and was in fact badly undermined by the huge American presence. The responsibility for securing that political base lay with the South Vietnamese.

The fundamental strategic mistake in Vietnam was the large-scale commitment of American ground forces as such. The commitment was not commensurate with the interests at stake; the failure to understand that at the outset was a political error, and it overshadows all the military blunders of the war, large and small. For however those ground forces might have been employed, the Communists would have been able to inflict large casualties on American units while simultaneously limiting their own. Given the disparity in willpower between the two sides, all the alternative ground-force strategies, like the one that was followed, would have probably led to withdrawal and defeat.

Two other factors must be borne in mind when we assess the postwar operational record of the American military. One is the standing difficulty of a global power — the need to contend with a wide range of contingencies, often on the spur of the moment, and often on behalf of interests that, though real, are of secondary importance. These constraints have a tendency to dilute expertise and to make realistic planning difficult. Another is the nature of war itself. In his famous remarks on "friction" in war, Clausewitz noted that in war the simplest things are difficult, and though critics of the military's operational performance often remind us of his injunction, they tend to forget it in their assessment of particular operations, where a standard of perfection is erected that is both retrospective and seriously misleading.

None of these factors excuses professional failure, but each forces us to adopt a more realistic standard in measuring professionalism, and by this more realistic standard the postwar operational performance of the military looks much better. Nevertheless, the existence of separate services and the weakness of the joint institutions that have been expected to supply cross-service expertise have had a deleterious effect on operational excellence. Under the system that prevailed until 1986, the chairman of the Joint Chiefs of Staff had little real power to enforce decisions on recalcitrant members. Perhaps even more important, the Joint Staff that served the JCS was composed of officers who later returned to duty with their own services and were not rewarded for joint positions. The individual services often held on to their most talented officers, whose careers were normally within a single service. In the planning of operations, a committee system prevailed, which discouraged the clear delineations of power and responsibility indispensable to effective staff work.

The 1947 National Security Act, largely in deference to the Navy's fear of service unification, set the pattern for these arrangements. The first substantial attempt to overcome its inadequacies was made in the 1958 Defense Reorganization Act. In justifying the act, Eisenhower argued that "separate ground, sea, and air warfare is gone forever. If ever again we should be involved in war, we will fight it in all elements, with all Services, as one single concentrated effort."[14] In seeking to make peacetime preparatory and organizational activity conform to this fact, the act established a set of unified commands that were to exercise operational command over forces that would continue to be provided by the military services. The act, as Paul Hammond once observed, represented an attempt to press "the task force concept applied with such success in World War II to its logical conclusion," and it therefore sought to relegate the services to supporting functions "roughly equivalent to what the Army Service Forces and Army Ground Forces commands did in World War II." That objective, however, was not realized, largely because the 1958 act established both an "operational" and an "administrative" chain of command, the latter controlled by the individual services and including control over discipline, personnel, training, and logistics. The arrangements that came to prevail, as Samuel Huntington has noted, largely frustrated the intentions of the bill's framers: "Each subordinate component commander in a unified command is responsible to the CINC of his command on operational matters and to the chief of his service for everything else, which, in peacetime, is almost everything of importance."[15]

Though the deleterious impact of "servicism" on operational planning and execution is easily documented, its impact on strategic planning and force development is much more uncertain. Servicism — that is, a malady that "exalts the individual military service and accords it primacy within the military establishment"[16] — does exist. The continuing existence of separate military services makes it difficult for civilians to get dispassionate military advice on a range of strategic and budgetary matters that touch the interests of the individual services. Since the military services are natural rivals for the control of competing roles and resources, they cannot provide disinterested answers. The members of the Joint Chiefs of Staff, save the chairman, are essentially representatives of the services they head; and officers on the Joint Staff have in the past normally considered themselves representatives of their own services. For these reasons, the Joint Chiefs of Staff has been virtually incapable of rendering certain kinds of advice. It has been particularly deficient at recommending allocations of roles and missions among the services. Its budgetary advice — the number of divisions, carrier battle groups, and air wings required to support national objectives — has usually been sharply discounted by civilian policy makers, for the reason that the advice reflects monetary amounts that are the outcome of bargaining among the military services themselves and are well in excess of figures behind which a political consensus could form.[17]

The absence of an institution to provide unified military advice in matters of national strategy and force development has had an important impact on defense organization in the United States since World War II; perhaps its most important, though indirect and paradoxical, consequence has been to enhance the power of the civilian Secretaries of Defense. This was a gradual development, unforeseen at the outset. The legislation that laid the basis for the postwar military establishment provided the civilian secretary with a very small staff. James Forrestal, who was the architect of the 1947 National Security Act, had hoped that the Joint Chiefs of Staff would resolve some of the vexing budgetary and "roles and missions" disputes that were looming on the horizon, but it soon became evident that the JCS was incapable of doing so. The budgetary figure the JCS proposed for the Defense Department for fiscal year 1949, the first budget year during which the new arrangements functioned, was about $30 billion, over twice the $13 billion limit Truman had set for the military. The conflict between the Air Force and the Navy over the appropriate means of nuclear delivery against the Soviet Union, a conflict that centered on the alternative procurement of B-36 bombers or "supercarriers," showed just as clearly that the JCS would be incapable of arbitrating "roles and missions" disputes among the services.[18]

The outbreak of the Korean War dampened the problem of interservice rivalry, just as it eased the budgetary problem, by making far more funds available. With the end of the war, however, the same two problems that had vexed Forrestal continually recurred. The competition between the Air Force and the Army over the control of an intermediate-range ballistic missile (the Thor-Jupiter dispute), and a similar rivalry over the control of Continental Air Defense, were only two among many striking instances of interservice rivalry during the decade. This rivalry was heightened by Eisenhower's unwillingness to entertain "split papers" from the JCS. Though civilian authorities imposed budgetary ceilings on each of the services, moreover, the services all enjoyed a great deal of autonomy in composing their own budgets.[19]

It was with the conviction that the division of the military into separate departments had introduced profound distortions in the American defense establishment that Robert McNamara assumed the office of the Secretary of Defense in 1961. McNamara sought to overcome these distortions not by creating a unified military staff but by centralizing power in the office of the Secretary of Defense. He conceived his role as that of an "active manager," not an umpire adjudicating the claims of the separate services. The claim reflected the Kennedy administration's view not only that the services strove to perform the same glamorous roles, thus resulting in an extraordinary amount of "waste" and "duplication," but also that the choices the services presented to civilian superiors as a consequence of this rivalry were frequently inadequate. Defense decision making required not only cutting out the duplication, but adding capabilities, like airlift and sealift, that had theretofore been neglected. A rational system of decision making also required a new budgetary system. Before McNamara arrived at the Pentagon, defense budgeting and military strategy "were treated as almost independent activities. They were carried out by different people, at different times, with different means of reference, and without a method for integrating their activities. The strategy and forces were thought to be essentially military matters, while the budget was thought to be mainly a civilian matter."[20] The consequences of this artificial separation between strategic and budgetary matters, according to most critics, were pernicious: under Eisenhower, Clark Murdock has argued, "the services were free to allocate their share of the constrained budget total — free to retain conflicting doctrines, construct duplicating weapons systems, deemphasize interdependent missions, and ignore less glamorous roles."[21]

There was much in the McNamara critique that was exaggerated; at the least, there was a tendency to attribute the force posture the Kennedy administration inherited in 1961 to institutional factors, whereas the real reason was the Eisenhower administration's strategic outlook — with which, of course, the Kennedy administration was profoundly unsympathetic. The shortage of strategic mobility assets (both airlift and sealift) for moving general-purpose forces to overseas theaters, the unwillingness of the Air Force to provide close support for Army units, concentrating instead on nuclear missions, the lack of material reserves for a prolonged conventional war — all these resulted primarily from the Eisenhower administration's "new look" in military strategy, with its emphasis on nuclear retaliation. These choices may have been wrong — it was the Kennedy administration's view that they were profoundly wrong — but it was civilian direction and not institutional deformity that provided the primary basis for them.[22]

It remains true that there were a number of areas in which the McNamara critique made a great deal of sense. The services had developed a vast array of nuclear systems, not all of which could be economically procured. The Kennedy administration poured resources into some programs (like ballistic missiles and nuclear submarines) and eliminated a number of others, with effects that on the whole were salutary. It may have exaggerated the deformities created by the Eisenhower administration's budgetary system, but there is little question that the Pentagon did require a centralized system for estimating budgets and for projecting them over much longer periods than had been customary. The Planning, Programming, and Budgeting System (PPBS) that McNamara introduced, though not without problems of its own, was for these reasons an improvement on what had gone before.

The most enduring legacy of the McNamara reign at the Pentagon was the increased power he gave to the office of the Secretary of Defense; his success in doing so, when placed alongside the failure of the 1958 Reorganization Act to create truly unified military commands, largely shaped the pattern of defense organization for the next two decades. The Secretary of Defense, now as then, has available to him a powerful set of institutional procedures by which to remake military policy, and though none of his successors has employed the powers of the office quite as extensively as McNamara did, there has been little temptation to revert to the prior order of things, even under Secretary Weinberger. The Reagan administration has sought to decentralize many decisions, and it has certainly allowed the service chiefs (and their civilian secretaries) wider discretion than was customary under Harold Brown or even Melvin Laird. But the critical decisions on force structure and strategy have in fact been made, for better or worse, by the responsible civilian officials.

It is primarily because of the power of the civilian Secretary of Defense that strategic planning and force development have *not* by and large fallen victim to "servicism."[23] The view that servicism does predominate rests on an indictment very similar to the one McNamara brought against defense organization a generation ago, but the contemporary indictment is even less persuasive than his. In considering the prevalence of "servicism," it will not do to cite the many deficiencies of the Joint Chiefs of Staff. These deficiencies, though real, are not of great significance in force planning and strategic development, for the reason that the advice of the JCS in such matters is "generally irrelevant, normally unread, and almost always disregarded."[24] Nor will it do to point to certain alleged deficiencies in the U.S. force structure — such as the underfunding of capabilities for rapid deployment, airlift, and sealift — and attribute them to the excessive influence of servicism. Decisions on these matters have long been made by civilians. It was the Congress that killed the major sealift program of the 1960s, the Fast Deployment Logistics Ship, believing it would make interventions of the Vietnam variety easier to undertake; and it was a Congress scandalized by the cost overruns on the C-5 that forced an early termination of that program as well. Similarly, there was no rapid deployment capability during the 1970s because no administration pushed for it. Although the 1977 directive of PD-18 called for the creation of a "rapid deployment force of several light divisions supported by sufficient air and sea lift to deal with Third World contingencies, particularly in Southwest Asia," the Carter administration did not take this requirement seriously until the final year of its term. Its attitude reflected a political outlook toward intervention in general, not the excessive influence of the services.

The most common evidence brought forth to demonstrate the detrimental influence of servicism is the number of areas where the services appear to duplicate each other's functions, such as

— different fighter aircraft for the Air Force (F-15 and F-16) and the Navy (F-14 and F-18);
— different close-support aircraft for the Air Force (A-10), the Navy (A-7), the Marine Corps (the AV-8A Harrier), and the Army (the Apache attack helicopter);
— the range of systems whose function is to gain aerial superiority, such as surface-to-air guns and missiles for the Army (Patriot, DIVAD, Chaparral), fighter aircraft (F-15 and F-16) designed for air-to-air combat, or bombers (F-111, F-15E) and surface-to-surface missile systems whose objective is enemy air bases.

The assumption of many critics is that most such duplication is waste. Yet that assumption ignores the extent to which military systems that appear to duplicate each other's functions can often operate synergistically to produce a military effect greater than the sum of their parts. Attacking aircraft that face a diverse array of threats to their survival find their evasive options progressively reduced, a danger well illustrated by the dense array of Soviet surface-to-air systems — each having a different performance envelope — that have magnified the threat to the manned bomber. Eliminating duplication may in some instances improve efficiency (by permitting, for instance, larger rates of production), but invariably the savings come at a price. The potential loss in military effectiveness is the most important competing consideration, but it is not the only one. Other dangers include a narrowing of the defense industrial base (as less efficient plants are shut down) and a reduction in government's bargaining power with defense contractors (as competitive pressures are reduced).[25] The critics, to be sure, may be right in arguing that "servicism" creates a bias toward duplication of effort. They have not been able to show, however, that effects of such duplication are in the main harmful, and in that respect the critique is misleading.

The one area where there does appear to be far too much redundancy is strategic nuclear systems — that is, precisely the area of defense policy where civilian influence is greatest. The services did not force the Reagan administration to revive the B-1, fight for the MX, plan for the Midgetman, develop air-, ground-, and sea-launched cruise missiles, or build Trident submarines and the extremely accurate D-5 missiles to go with them (to say nothing of its expensive research into the feasibility of a defense against nuclear attack). If it was madness to do all these things, it was preeminently civilian, not military madness; the services could have been made to accept a much different program with relative ease.

STRATEGIC PLURALISM AND PRESIDENTIAL LEADERSHIP

There is no question that the two great divisions on both sides of the civil-military divide — between president and Congress and among the military services — have powerful structural consequences. On the civilian side, they make military policy subject to potent special interests, and much of the inefficiency characteristic of the defense establishment is attributable to that factor. On the military side, "servicism" has held a particularly baleful effect on the conduct of operations. Whether that defect has been overcome by the 1986 Defense Reorganization Act remains to be seen.

The effect on national strategy and force development produced by the dual division is much more difficult to characterize. Divided civilian institutions and divided services do make for "strategic pluralism" — that is, "the possession of a wide variety of forces and weapons to meet a diversity of potential security threats."[26] The pattern, however, has not been a constant one. Though normally Congress serves to increase the propensity toward strategic pluralism, in the 1980s it on balance served to weaken the tendency (through its skeptical attitude toward the pluralistic defense program of the Reagan administration). In many circumstances, moreover, pluralism is a desirable feature of national strategy; the duplication and redundancy it gives rise to in weapons systems and tactical concepts may unexpectedly prove of real military or political value.

There are, nevertheless, certain circumstances when the proliferation of strategic concepts becomes unwieldy — when the best, as it were, becomes the enemy of the good. During periods of fiscal stringency, the failure to prune strategic concepts may yield a force structure that is badly unbalanced or even hollow. As budgetary cuts are made across the board, unit costs for weapons systems are driven up, and the quality of the services' manpower base deteriorates as well. Under these conditions which prevailed in the late 1970s and will probably recur in the late 1980s and early 1990s, it becomes much more difficult for the services to modernize weapons systems efficiently, recruit and retain quality manpower, and keep their units in fighting trim. National strategy then comes to resemble the unformed character described by Randall Jarrell in *Pictures from an Institution* who, wanting to be all things to all men, ended by being nothing in particular.[27]

Under the American system of government, only the president is well positioned to make these difficult strategic choices. Congress is badly handicapped when it comes to doing so. It can block and check; but it has great difficulty in formulating a coherent alternative. Nor can the military provide the stimulus for basic changes in national strategy, for reasons that go beyond the narrowly institutional. The military lacks the criteria to make such choices, even were it capable of speaking with a unified voice. A system that depends so heavily on presidential guidance when difficult choices must be made is going to find itself in trouble when the occupant of the presidency is unwilling to make them, and that is precisely the situation that characterized the Reagan administration. Confronted with the prospect of a period of relative famine in defense expenditures, the administration persistently refused in the mid-1980s to prune the lush growth of strategic concepts it had encouraged earlier in the decade. That refusal, in turn, heightened the tendency toward strategic pluralism inherent in our defense organization.

Still, one may legitimately wonder whether the defect was primarily institutional or political — whether it stemmed, that is, from inherent defects in our institutional arrangements, as many have charged, or from the flawed political vision of President Reagan and Secretary Weinberger. It is, in fact, the latter explanation that appears more persuasive. The Reagan administration has had ample tools to curb strategic pluralism and force difficult decisions on the Pentagon and the Congress. What it has lacked is the will and desire to do so.

Of all postwar administrations, that of President Reagan has been the most pluralistic in matters of national strategy. Its insistence on capabilities allowing for the commitment of American ground and air forces in Western Europe, Southwest Asia, and South Korea (the three-war strategy); its call for a strategy of "horizontal escalation" that would allow for American counteroffensives against the enemy's vulnerable points outside the theater where aggression took place; its return to the "long war" standard of the 1960s; its desire to reestablish a condition of undisputed American naval superiority; its support for the "Deep Strike" initiatives and "Follow on Forces Attack" sponsored by General Bernard Rogers, Supreme Allied Commander in Europe; its refusal to renounce the possibility that American nuclear weapons might be used first in response to a Soviet conventional attack, combined with a reluctance to rely on this possibility for deterrence; finally, its dream of one day rendering nuclear weapons "impotent and obsolete" through the development and deployment of strategic defenses — all these doctrines, considered together, reflect a condition of strategic pluralism run amok. It was well beyond American resources to take all these ideas with equal seriousness even in the early days of the administration, when its defense program enjoyed substantial support in Congress and from public opinion; the decline of such support in the mid-1980s left an extraordinary gap between the administration's declaratory policies and the resources available for the defense budget.

No institutional necessity compelled the administration to embrace all these strategic doctrines. Its strategic pluralism stemmed not from its decentralized approach to defense management but rather from intellectual conviction. This is plainly so if we contrast the pattern that prevailed under Reagan with that of the two previous Republican administrations in 1953–61 and 1969–77. In the Eisenhower and Nixon-Ford periods, defense management was largely decentralized, as it has been under Reagan. The detailed review of the services' favored weapons systems, characteristic of the McNamara era, was absent under Eisenhower and was abandoned under Nixon. Melvin Laird, Secretary of Defense from 1969 to 1973, patched up the rocky relations between civilians and the service chiefs that had existed under the Kennedy and Johnson administrations. Substantial latitude was given to the chiefs of the individual services to shape their own programs. Strategic doctrine, however, was far less pluralistic, and this had a restraining effect on budget levels in all the services, particularly the Army. Both Eisenhower and Nixon sharply cut ground forces, and though this was partially due to withdrawal from the two great Asian land wars of the postwar period, it also reflected the belief that the commitment of American ground forces to conflicts like Korea and Vietnam would be a losing proposition for the United States in the future.

The power of the civilian Secretaries of Defense, and by extension the president, has of course not been constant in the postwar era. In the 1970s, room for maneuvering at the Pentagon was much less than it had been for McNamara. With the general decline in defense spending (in real terms), civilian officials at DOD had their hands full ensuring force readiness, modernizing existing units, and retaining an effective manpower base. In retrospect, it appears that the defense budget as a whole was seriously underfunded — as the Reagan administration persuasively charged at the outset of its term. But Secretary of Defense Weinberger has faced few such constraints. The substantial increase in defense funding that occurred from 1981 to 1985 — with cumulative growth amounting to $329.5 billion — gave the administration considerable latitude in shaping the force posture. That it failed to use this power to create a coherent defense program — that it exacerbated rather than curbed the underlying tendency toward strategic pluralism — was a political, not an institutional, failing.

3 · Some Organizational Dilemmas

It has long been recognized that an appropriate pattern of civil-military relations requires some attention to the fact that the military services are extremely large organizations. Over two million men and women are in uniform, and the influence of the services reaches far beyond that. The theorist of civil-military relations must therefore be concerned with a set of issues that go beyond those involving the level, scope, and unity of civilian and military authority. Of those issues, three stand out in importance: whether organizations should be structured along purposive or functional lines; the appropriate degree of centralization (or decentralization); and responsiveness to change. The last two are examined in this chapter; the first is considered in chapter 5 in the context of proposals to reorganize the Department of Defense.

Centralized Oversight and Decentralized Initiative

The problem of centralization is best understood as one of competing virtues (or vices), for there must be some measure of both centralized oversight and decentralized initiative in any organization; to carry one or the other principle to an extreme normally leads to pernicious consequences. The degree of centralization will affect the extent to which accurate or misleading information is transmitted from higher to lower echelons and vice versa; and the character and effectiveness of any organization, in turn, will be affected by the specificity of the orders given to lower units as well as the amount of initiative expected from them. As Martin van Creveld has observed, an ideal command system, like any organization,

> should be able to gather information accurately, continuously, comprehensively, selectively, and fast. Reliable means must be developed to distinguish the true from the false, the relevant from the irrelevant, the material from the immaterial. . . . Orders should be clear and unambiguous; they must tell

subordinates everything they should know, but nothing more. Monitoring should be close enough to secure reliable execution, but not so close as to undermine the authority and choke the initiative (or even, as sometimes happens, the very ability to act) of subordinate commanders at all levels.[1]

These issues, moreover, are relevant to both military administration and military operations. The problems that arose in the reform of the War and Navy departments at the turn of the century were examined earlier from the standpoint of what spheres of decision it was appropriate to vest in civilian and military officials, but these problems can be understood in organizational terms as well. The basic difficulties raised by administration of the Navy Department at the turn of the century, as Leonard White has written, revolved around a universal problem of administrative organization,

> how to delegate adequate authority to bureaus to enable them to act with initiative and energy, and at the same time reserve enough authority in the responsible agency head to ensure coordination, subordination, and responsibility. The navy suffered on the one hand from overpowerful bureaus, each jealously guarding its respective prerogatives, unwilling to yield authority to secure coordination, professionally arrogant, and unmindful of the needs of the Department as such; and on the other hand from the correlative vice of Secretaries whose talents were at times deficient and whose office was inadequately staffed to enable them to exercise the powers of control that were nominally those of the Secretary of the Navy.[2]

In the conduct of operations, issues arise that are very similar to those we encounter in administration. This is true despite the fact that the element of danger in military operations demands personal qualities wholly different from those required in military administration. In their masterly study *The Israeli Army*, Edward Luttwak and Dan Horowitz pose the problem of command and control in terms analogous to those suggested by White:

> In the midst of battle, the subordinate commander at the head of his troops may see only a narrow segment of the fighting; his superiors at higher headquarters in the rear will have a far broader picture of the tactical situation, but one lacking in immediacy. In the flux of combat with its fleeting opportunities and sudden dangers, much depends on how quickly an army can respond — and this in turn depends on the *level* at which tactical decisions are made: the lower the echelon of decision, the nearer to the scene of battle and the faster the response.[3]

In both operations and administration, excessive centralization will suffocate initiative at lower levels; it may even induce what the sociologists call "dysfunctional" behavior — that is, behavior calculated to frustrate the overall purposes of the organization. Excessive decentralization, on the other hand, can lead to a mass of uncoordinated activity, all to no apparent purpose, sound and fury signifying nothing. The history of warfare provides plenty of instances of the latter, characteristic of ages of primitive communications. The advanced state of modern communications, however, more commonly gives rise to the former problem, for it allows commanders — both civilian and military — to reach down to absurdly low levels in the chain of command.

Excessive centralization afflicted both administrative practices and military operations during the war in Vietnam. Field units lacked organic logistics support and depended instead on Logistics Command Centers all around the Pacific basin. The system, as van Creveld has argued, "was dependent on constant, detailed communications between the Logistic Command Centers and the outfits in the field and, furthermore, on the former's ability to develop and maintain a statistical model of the latter's requirements." Despite the complexity and sophistication of the requisition system, it was overwhelmed by the vast amounts of information it needed to function effectively. "Instead of using information to fine-tune the relationship between supply and demand, units were forced to send back men (the stationary Logistic Command Centers, with no permanent ties to any single outfits, insisted that the field come to the rear instead of vice versa) to walk over acres of stores and depots as far away as Okinawa and pick up whatever was needed." The inefficiencies that resulted from these procedures were, of course, the consequence of previous attempts to ensure maximum efficiency by doing away with the slack resources inherent in a less centralized system.[4]

The most famous instance of highly centralized arrangements during the Vietnam era was the conduct of the air war. Under the Democrats, the bombing campaigns over North Vietnam were orchestrated entirely from Washington, generating a tremendous demand for information from the field. Bombing targets were selected at the famous Tuesday luncheons at the White House, at which no military officer was present until 1967 — when a congressional investigation brought the practice to light.[5] The interference in operational details was typical of the Democratic administrations of the 1960s, and there were occasions on which it may well have been justified. The request that the ships participating in the quarantine of Cuba in 1962 draw closer to the island so as to give the Soviet Union more time to consider its response was an instance of neither excessive centralization nor improper intrusion on the Navy's sphere of responsibility. Whatever the merit of the request, it had a clear political rationale and involved considerations beyond the ken of those whose professional responsibility it was to run the blockade.[6]

The detailed control civilians exercised over the conduct of the air war in Vietnam had no such justification. The Johnson administration wanted to intimidate the North Vietnamese and to demonstrate American resolve; but it also wanted to reassure China and the Soviet Union about the limited nature of American aims. These objectives did not reinforce one another; they canceled each other out. Unable to articulate a coherent political strategy for the bombing, the administration nevertheless exercised minute control over the smallest tactical details. The story is emblematic of the entire conduct of the Vietnam War. Though those who ran the war from Washington were forced to delegate responsibility to field commanders on most matters, the civilians surrendered this right with great reluctance and often made decisions on a multitude of petty details. On the most important matters, however, the administration was silent and indeed deeply confused. It saw nothing peculiar in taking on itself the right to decide whether antipersonnel rounds should be used in the defense of Khe Sanh in 1968, but it was incapable of articulating an intelligent strategy for the prosecution of the war.[7]

Of all the charges that have been brought against the McNamara Pentagon, indeed, that of excessive centralization is the most persuasive. The one common theme that unites the McNamara era is his unwillingness or inability to delegate responsibility. Partly this propensity arose from his distrust of — and at times even contempt for — the advice of the uniformed military, partly from excessive faith in his own powers. But it is not surprising in these circumstances that civil-military relations deteriorated sharply during his tenure or that much of the interaction between civilians and military bordered on the pathological. This inability to delegate responsibility, in turn, is the feature of the whole story that still seems the most remarkable, for in retrospect we know that the arrogance it reflected was somewhat less than fully justified and that some measure of humility would not have been inappropriate.

Expertise and Innovation

The military displays three characteristics that entitle it to be considered a profession: corporateness, expertise, and responsibility.[8] Not all professions share these qualities to the same degree, and they are not of equal significance in each. But they are present to at least some degree in all, and it is impossible to understand the proper role of the military aside from them. Corporateness sets the military apart from the rest of society; it also forges the moral bonds that are indispensable to its effectiveness in war. A sense of responsibility is equally vital, for without it there would be a profound contradiction — as there is for many societies — between the requirements of external security and internal freedom. The existence of this danger was a staple element in early Anglo-American analyses of the danger posed by standing armies, and it maintained a large measure of political appeal through most of American history.[9] That the United States has managed since World War II to maintain a large military establishment in peacetime without seriously compromising its free institutions is a notable accomplishment. Though we now take it virtually for granted, we ought not to forget that it was long thought impossible.

The most problematic of these professional qualities is expertise. The attempt made earlier in this work to allocate spheres of authority to civilians and the military in strategy, operations, and administration may be understood primarily as an attempt to define the character of the military's expertise; it is apparent, however, that the assumption this theory rests on — that the military does in fact possess the expertise the theory assigns to it — may not be well founded in particular cases. Indeed, there are many theorists who argue that the military organization is normally hostile to innovation and, save in exceptional circumstances, is incapable of adapting to change. Its outdated expertise, moreover, may have catastrophic consequences.

Because of the complexity of tasks it must perform and the specialized knowledge it requires, the military is necessarily organized bureaucratically. Like other large organizations, it makes use of a division of labor; and it perforce relies upon specialized agencies, bureaus, and commands to research promising new scientific and technological concepts, develop new weaponry, train new recruits, test the interaction of men and machines in realistic settings, and finally, lead vast groupings of soldiers in war. It is a typical observation of organizational theorists that those at the bottom of an administrative hierarchy do not necessarily share the perspective of those at the top: they are able to see only a small portion of a problem at any given time, and they rely upon standard operating procedures to communicate with one another. Frequently a certain resistance to change develops that arises partly from inertia and partly because innovation disturbs existing practices and may constitute a fundamental threat to the organization's (or suborganization's) raison d'être.[10]

Decision processes as often as not are best understood in terms of not an analytic but a cybernetic paradigm. The former posits that, in reaching a decision, "a number of alternatives will be conceived, with consideration given to the probable outcome of each; that relevant goals will be integrated as an *intrinsic* part of the decision process; that the process will seek out and respond to new information; and finally, that the alternative chosen will be the one with the highest probable net payoff in terms of the decision maker's goals." The cybernetic paradigm, on the other hand, assumes that large, complex organizations will do none of these things. Its model of the decision process is not unlike servomechanisms, such as thermostats, that perform no output calculations but merely "track a few feedback variables and react solely to the variations in this select information. In all other respects, they are essentially blind to the environment. They have a repertory of operations which they perform in sequence while monitoring the few feedback variables."[11]

There are plenty of examples one might point to in illustrating the hold organizational routines have had over military establishments in the twentieth century. The horse cavalry survived World War I even though it was useless in an age of tanks and machine guns; battleships survived even though the increasing weight of evidence favored the aircraft carrier. The infantry charge was revived in the years before World War I at a time when technological developments were pointing the other way, some clearly demonstrated in the Russo-Japanese War of 1904–5; indeed, the massed infantry assault charge was to persist well into World War I despite considerable evidence of its disproportionate cost. The Air Force resisted the introduction of the ICBM, seeing in it a threat to the manned bomber; the Army had the M-16 forced upon it by a coalition of outsiders in the Air Force and the Office of the Secretary of Defense despite substantial evidence that the M-16 was clearly superior to its rival the M-14. And perhaps the most famous and resonant example is the failure of the French army to keep abreast of changes in the art of warfare before the outbreak of World War II, a failure that would have profound consequences.[12]

To be sure, there is a sense in which these examples are partially misleading, drawn as many of them are from an age in which the importance of technological change was as yet imperfectly understood. The undeniable importance of technological development in accounting for the outcome of World War II — whether in the development of radar, the airplane, or the atomic bomb — has transformed generals and admirals "from being the most traditional element in any national society — hanging on to their horses, or their sailing ships, for as long as possible — into the boldest innovators."[13] Yet even in its innovation, organizational theorists assert, the military tends for the most part to follow predictable lines, to seek improvements on existing forms that require no radical organizational or doctrinal changes. This is one of the central assertions of the military reformers, and whatever its validity, it is in no way inconsistent with the argument of the organizational theorists.

There is a further sense in which military establishments run the risk of promoting weapons that will not work in combat and adhering to doctrines out of touch with the state of contemporary warfare. They do not have the unpleasant though in some respects salutary experience of a continuing and regular check on their precepts. Failure in war may register sufficient shock to force a military organization to engage in an agonizing reappraisal of its basic tenets — as may the failure of an allied army — but the lessons taught by contemporary wars are often obscure and in any case are episodic. The business corporation, though it may suffer from modes of decision making even more irrational than those the military falls victim to, at least has an external check in profitability that will limit the discretionary power of management, and there is a continuing check imposed by consumer preferences that not even the largest advertising budgets can alter.*

An important, though often neglected, implication of organization theory is that the same characteristics that hinder innovations in military organizations also make such organizations resistant to change

---

* The importance of external checks in altering organizational routines is apparent from a number of disputes in economic theory. Milton Friedman, in "The Methodology of Positive Economics," in *Essays on Positive Economics* (Chicago: University of Chicago Press, 1971), made the paradoxical assertion that economic theory was valuable precisely to the degree that it was descriptively inaccurate. The theory of the firm proposed by the classical economists was superior, in his view, to that put forward by Richard Cyert and James March in *A Behavioral Theory of the Firm* (Englewood Cliffs, N.J.: Prentice Hall, 1963) because of its greater predictive power. This greater power, in Friedman's view, stems from the existence of external checks, largely imposed by consumer preference, that force the firm to modify its organizational routines.

Anticipated or actual failure in war is the external check that is largely responsible for change in military organizations. Because major wars occur infrequently and because minor wars (as in Lebanon or the Falklands) offer ambiguous lessons, it follows that balance-of-power theory is a less powerful predictive guide to change in military organizations than classical economic theory is to change in the business corporation. The competing claims of the balance of power and organizational theorists are examined in Posen, *Sources of Military Doctrine*, passim, and in Kenneth N. Waltz, *Theory of International Politics* (Reading, Mass.: Addison-Wesley, 1979). And see also the argument, running along parallel lines, between John Kenneth Galbraith, *The Affluent Society* (Boston: Houghton Mifflin, 1955), and F. A. Hayek, "The Non-sequitur of the 'Dependence Effect,'" in *Studies in Philosophy, Politics and Economics* (New York: Simon and Schuster, 1967), pp. 313–17.

imposed "from the outside." That such organizations exist at all means they serve a critical function, even if they are not performing it well for the moment. Outsiders may force a service to accept a certain decision, but the service must be relied upon to implement it. Issues like the development of a major weapons system, moreover, are never settled with a single stroke of the pen. The interval between the perception of a need (or "requirement") for a weapon and its actual deployment with the troops is usually very long, especially in the United States; and military organizations may have significantly greater staying power than their civilian superiors, whose terms of office expire and whose perspectives change. The organization will have control over information (which it may be reluctant to pass on to hostile outsiders); it will have access to technical data that outsiders lack the resources or the expertise to dispute. McNamara's creation of the systems analysis office in DOD was intended to provide the civilian secretary with such an independent source of military advice, but even the resources of the whiz kids were limited. The resistance to outside pressure will become particularly acute if the military organization feels its autonomy is being challenged; for to the knowledge that its prerogatives are being usurped has to be added the inescapable indignity that it is considered incompetent.

The experience of the McNamara revolution illustrates many of these issues with some clarity. McNamara, among other things, forced the Air Force and the Navy to procure a joint fighter, encouraged (with the vigorous support of his president) an understanding of counterinsurgency warfare in the Army; pushed for the development of airmobile concepts centered on the helicopter; insisted that the Air Force procure the F-4 fighter and the A-7 attack plane (which had both been originally developed by the Navy), and with the support of Air Force Chief of Staff Curtis LeMay, spurred the Army to accept a limited purchase of the AR-15 (later M-16) rifle.

Most of these initiatives represented reasonable exertions of civilian power, though not all enjoyed equal success. The civilian insistence that the Air Force accept the F-4 and the A-7, an attempt to curb unnecessary duplication, was perhaps the most successful of all these initiatives. The Navy, however, was able to resist successfully the acquisition of the F-111, in part because the special requirements of carrier operations gave it an argument that civilians lacked the technical expertise to rebut. The Secretary of Defense in effect forced the Army to acquire limited numbers of the M-16, but he had to rely on the Army's technical bureaus to "develop" the weapon, with unfortunate results. McNamara was greatly aided in the 1962 decision to procure a limited number of M-16s by the fact that the rifle had the vigorous support of LeMay, and ultimately the Army as a whole came round to accepting the weapon not because of civilian pressure but because the combatant commander in Vietnam, William Westmoreland, became a vigorous sponsor of it.[14] The airmobile concept caught on well within the Army because it enjoyed the support of the powerful airborne faction, whose members included Westmoreland, Taylor, Ridgway, and Gavin. Counterinsurgency, by contrast, was a "bureaucratic orphan"—opposed by the military because it was "incompatible with their conception of professionalism. The essence of counterinsurgency theory," as Richard Betts has observed, "was paramilitary civic action, a delicate interweaving of political and military functions—the kind of fusion that irritated so many of the military elite who preferred a clear line of demarcation between the two spheres. The ideal Green Beret was supposed to be ambassador, propagandist, medical and economic aide, applied anthropologist, and surrogate ward heeler for the client government."*

That military organizations have the resources and incentive to resist and frustrate change forced upon them "from the outside" ought at least to make us wary of the attempt. It serves, on the whole, to reestablish the presumption in favor of deferring to the professional expertise of the military in matters that concern its professional function—a presumption most organizational theorists have sought to demolish. It also points to three other factors that ought to be borne in mind in the contemporary debate over defense reform. One is the value of services whose functions in some degree overlap and that are therefore competitive with one another. Another is the danger that civilian intervention, over time, will reflect a variety of inconsistent proposals and may work at cross-purposes. And the third is the importance of effecting reform at least partly "from the inside"—that is, through promotion rather than continual outside pressure.

Though duplication of function is often condemned by civilians, it does constitute a valuable check on the intellectual rigidities that military organizations are subject to. Interservice rivalry flourished in the late 1940s and 1950s, and it provided civilians with a range of information and a menu of choices they would not have had if they had faced a monolithic military establishment. The services all showed little hesita-

---

*Betts, *Statesmen, Soldiers, and Cold War Crises*, p. 130 and chap. 7, passim. In retrospect, it is difficult to know which side was more grievously wrong in Vietnam—the civilians, who failed to understand that building political support for the South Vietnamese government was something the Vietnamese had to do for themselves, or the military, who believed that all the United States had to do was "kill more Vietcong," and who sent American units thrashing about the countryside with enormous firepower and destructive political effect.

tion in questioning the professional military judgment of their rivals in the other service arms, and the consequence was a vigorous and bracing debate on national strategy that was forced up to the civilian level for resolution. Soon after McNamara entered office, such interservice rivalry sharply declined. The services, conscious of the challenge to military professionalism that McNamara was undertaking, became reluctant to provide civilians with yet more ammunition to impinge upon their areas of professional responsibility, and on most questions the Joint Chiefs of Staff came to form a common front against him. This was the origin of the pattern of "logrolling" that came to characterize the deliberations of the Joint Chiefs, a pattern very different from the interservice rivalries it supplanted.[15]

The corporate and bureaucratic character of the services makes them fairly predictable organizations, and while that can lead to unfortunate consequences, it also provides a measure of continuity to defense policy. Civilian power, on the other hand, is more widely diffused. Lacking any corporate identity relevant to military policy, civilian critics — particularly in the Congress and the news media — will invariably develop a wide variety of proposals to reform the military that are inconsistent with each other. Civilian intervention, if it becomes habitual and extends to details, will more often than not reflect no guiding intelligence and may work at cross-purposes — tendencies powerfully reinforced by the separation of powers and the general diffusion of influence characteristic of the American governing system.

This danger may be illustrated by taking as examples two editorials that appeared in the *New York Times* and the *Wall Street Journal* in 1983. Both were sharply critical of the military. We learned from the *Times* that the services' "high technology procures advantages that look impressive on paper but are only marginally useful in battle" and that the "fighting in Lebanon and the Falklands has underlined that it is skills and tactics, not technology, that win wars, and that simple weapons perform better than complex systems." "Through its addiction to complex technology," the *Times* concluded, "the Pentagon seems willing to sacrifice both quantity and effectiveness for weapons of unbearable cost and dubious advantage." From the *Wall Street Journal*, on the other hand, we found that the Reagan administration "needs to knock the services' heads together and force them to come to grips with the lessons of recent conflicts, in which it was clear that technology is rapidly changing the battlefield environment."[16] Both editorial pages agreed, in other words, that the American armed services had not come to terms with the "lessons of battle" and were perhaps incapable of doing so. No one seemed to notice or care that the lessons drawn by our two leading national newspapers were totally at odds with one another and had radically different implications for the doctrine, tactics, and technology of the American services.

The belief that all this head knocking will lead to fruitful consequences in the long run is apparently widely held among civilian elites, but it is of dubious merit. The predictable consequence is that the marbles one set of civilians tries to empty out of the services' heads will in all likelihood be put back in by others, and the turbulence all this change induces in the military will make it less formidable in peace and less effective in war. If intellectual fashion changed as swiftly in military circles as it does in the civilian world, long-range planning would be even more difficult than it now is. It is doubtful that the consequences would be wholly beneficial.

These organizational considerations also indicate that the way military reform is pursued will have an important bearing on its success. If civilians are persuaded that the highest level of an officer corps is incompetent, reform ought to proceed through the promotion, to the highest levels of the affected service, of men committed to change. If there are no such men — or none with sufficient weight among their fellow officers to command the respect to get things done — then it is likely that will reflect on the advisability of the reform program as a whole. It will certainly reduce the likelihood that the program will be implemented in anything like the spirit in which it was conceived.

The history of civil-military relations in America is full of examples in which civilian leadership reached down into the services and plucked from obscurity military men who went on to enjoy illustrious careers at or near the top of their services. Lincoln did it with his generals until he found the formidable combination of talents embodied in the officership of Grant and Sherman. Theodore Roosevelt afforded protection to then captain William S. Sims. To Franklin Roosevelt we owe the appointment of George C. Marshall, who entered office at a time when the nation desperately needed a man of strategic comprehension and organizational genius in the office of the Chief of Staff. In our own day, President Carter gave the reins of the Army to Edward C. Meyer, whose judicious appointment did much to revive the morale of his service. All these examples show that, through the appointment power, civilians can play a central role in the governance of the services; they also show that alongside these inspired choices went the delegation of responsibility and authority. All successful and enduring military reforms in the past have had this as a hallmark. For in the end it cannot be otherwise.

Perhaps the central issue in civil-military relations is therefore not one of authority or expertise but one of responsibility. There is no substitute for an officer corps in which the civilian leadership of the country can place its confidence. If that officer corps is a bad one, reforms imposed from the outside will likely come to nothing — or worse. If the weapons procurements sponsored by this officer corps reflect a profound misunderstanding of the nature of warfare, its education will not be furthered by forcing upon it weapons that it does not believe in and that reflect operational concepts it considers fundamentally wrong. It will either reject them or — if this fails — mold them to its own purposes, and the result may be something that is satisfactory to neither the military nor the civilians nor the nation as a whole.

The great reform of the American Army that took place at the turn of the century under Elihu Root was informed by an understanding of this character. The changes Root proposed were far reaching. It is notable, however, that the basic thrust of the reforms was to concentrate a divided responsibility in the office of the Chief of Staff. After the disgraceful performance of the Army in the Spanish-American War, this might seem in retrospect a peculiar response, for all our contemporary political instincts go against it. Our solution would be to systematically strip the Army of the responsibility to decide matters that, on the evidence of the war, it had not handled wisely. Root understood that the critical deficiency the war had revealed in the organization of the Army was that its leadership had too little responsibility, not too much. This understanding was the centerpiece of the Root reforms, and his insight into this matter entitles him to be considered one of our greatest Secretaries of War.

THE BURDEN OF PROOF

The critical importance of institutional and organizational considerations in the governance of the military services does not mean these considerations can be determinative in every case. They merely establish a presumption in favor of deferring to the judgment of the military in those matters that concern its professional function. The military, for its part, has a corresponding duty to defer to its civilian superiors when questions of high policy or administrative efficiency arise. The presumption in favor of military expertise may be overridden in particular circumstances, but if in the normal course of affairs it is regularly and habitually overridden, something is seriously wrong with the pattern of civil-military relations. This presumption, as the McNamara revolution shows, still leaves civilian leaders with a wide charter. The classic rationales of civilian intervention afford a legitimate basis for far-reaching control over the services. The principles, of course, may be abused; the right of civilian superiority in political matters and the claim of military autonomy may be invoked in circumstances where they are not applicable. But the principles themselves are sound, and civil-military relations will become deranged if they are systematically disregarded.

Many will no doubt find unsatisfactory a solution to the problem of civil-military relations that relies so much on something as intangible as mutual deference. Yet this is scarcely a novel proposition in the history of institutional thought, and indeed the students of civil-military relations have much to learn from episodes in our constitutional history in which this consideration played a critical role. The most telling comparison is to be found in the attitude our greatest jurists adopted toward the exercise of judicial review. The reluctance of Holmes, Brandeis, and Frankfurter to overturn the constitutionally enacted judgments of legislative bodies stemmed from their appreciation that to do so on a regular basis would be incompatible with the basic presupposition of American constitutionalism, under which the people are considered to be self-governing. They wondered whether judges could see the future clearly enough to impose their own values on a "vast, complex, changeable society."[17] A comparable question might fairly be asked of civilians who propose to force innovation on military establishments. Remote from the inner workings of the military and removed from sources of technical information that ought in many instances to remain secret, civilian reformers are at a serious disadvantage. Accordingly, they must meet a heavy burden of proof if the civilian statesman is to repose his confidence in them.

There was yet a further danger in the exercise of judicial review, one equally relevant to the problem of civil-military relations. The exercise of the power of judicial review, James Bradley Thayer once wrote, "even when unavoidable, is always attended with a serious evil, namely, that the correction of legislative mistakes comes from the outside, and the people thus lose the political experience, and the moral education and stimulus that comes from fighting the question out in the ordinary way, and correcting their own errors. The tendency of a common and easy resort to this great function, now lamentably too common, is to dwarf the political capacity of the people, and to deaden its sense of moral responsibility. It is no light thing to do that."[18] The same considerations apply to an officer corps whose judgment is habitually disregarded and whose professional competence is regularly impugned. It may not lose political experience, to be sure; indeed, it is likely to try to recapture in the political arena all that it can of its privileges and prerogatives. It may lose, though, the habit of correcting its own mistakes. Most important, it may lose its best sense of itself — the conception of officership as an honorable employment. Honor is the *principle* of an officer corps in the sense in which Montesquieu employed the term — that is, it is the sentiment indispensable to its successful functioning.[19] An officer corps that is treated as a collection of incompetents will attract men with a mean and narrow spirit; and by an insidious process of self-selection it will exclude those with the elevation of character we have a right to expect. This is a loss that cannot be measured by any material standard — save perhaps an increasing incidence of corruption — but it is in the end the most important one.

Occasionally, it is true, the presumption in favor of the military may be rebutted, the burden of proof may be met. The greatest conundrums of civil-military relations have often arisen at moments of supreme national peril, and in these circumstances the duty of civilian judgment cannot be escaped. Perhaps the most famous instance of this in the annals of warfare occurred on the Allied side during World War I, when David Lloyd George, prime minister of Britain, made his famous walk to the Admiralty and forced the Royal Navy to adopt the convoy system. This involved purely military considerations, for no one disputed the strategic importance of keeping the lifeline open. Whether the Navy would have instituted convoys in the absence of such intervention continues to be a subject of historical dispute, for Jellicoe, the First Sea Lord, seems to have arrived reluctantly at this conclusion a few days before. In this case, moreover, a group of younger officers in the Admiralty — and the American officer William S. Sims, for whom Jellicoe had high regard — had concluded that ocean convoy was indispensable if the desperate situation brought on by Germany's adoption of unrestricted submarine warfare was to be salvaged, and there consequently existed a powerful professional case against the Royal Navy's dogged adherence to "offensive" measures. It is nevertheless arguable that the final push toward the adoption of convoys had to be given by the civilian leadership of the country and that without such intervention the change would have occurred much later. Churchill was to comment bitterly that "the reluctance of all the naval chiefs in every Allied country to adopt convoys finds its counterpart only in the reluctance of the military chiefs of all the armies, Allied and enemy, to comprehend the significance of the tank. In both cases these means of salvation were forced upon them from outside and below."[20]

Whether we face such extraordinary circumstances today is the principal question raised by the contemporary movement for military reform. The central proposition of the reformers is that the American military, in Jeffrey Record's words, has been guilty of a pattern of "persistent professional malpractice that in any other profession would constitute grounds for disbarment, denial of tenure, or legal action."[21] Whatever the merit of the charge, the ground of dispute is at least clear. It revolves around the question whether the incompetence of the American military and its failure to fulfill its own professional function is so manifest as to subordinate the institutional and organizational imperatives arising from a principled statement of the appropriate relationship that ought to exist between civilians and the military.

II · The Call for Reform

4 · The Limitations of Military Reform

THE NATURE OF THE MILITARY REFORM MOVEMENT

It has become increasingly popular in the 1980s to argue that the critical deficiencies of American defense primarily lie not in the inadequacy of the resources devoted to defense but in the bankruptcy of the ideas that inform the organization, equipment, and employment of the American armed forces. There have been many variations on this theme, but no critics sounding it have been so persistent or so effective in making their case in the various organs of public opinion as the loosely affiliated group that has come to be known as the military reformers. Their critique of American military policy gained increasing numbers of adherents in the 1980s and at some point may play a crucial role in determining American defense policy. Reform themes have been championed by neoliberals like Gary Hart and neoconservative groups like the Heritage Foundation and indeed have been warmly received by writers all along the ideological spectrum – a fact that both invites interest and provokes suspicion.*

The following seven propositions appear to me to be central to the notion of military reform:

1. The Navy is organized around a potentially fatal tactical construct centered on the large-deck aircraft carrier. Reflecting a dogmatic rejec-

---

* Perhaps the best short introduction to the literature on military reform, apart from James Fallows' *National Defense*, are two publications sponsored by the Heritage Foundation. See Barlow, *Reforming the Military*, and Kuhn, "Department of Defense: Ending Defense Stagnation." Senator Hart's contributions to the reform debate reflect the influence of his assistant, William S. Lind. See Gary Hart, *America Can Win: The Case for Military Reform* (Bethesda, Md.: Adler and Adler, 1986); Hart, Taft, and Lind, *White Paper on Defense*; and other writings cited in the Bibliography.

The core group among the reformers includes John Boyd, Steven Canby, Pierre Sprey, William Lind, and Franklin Spinney. Jeffrey Record is a self-described "fellow traveler" of the reformers, and that is not a bad characterization of Edward Luttwak, who has best articulated a number of reform themes but whose thought is too wide-

tion of the possibilities of V/STOL aircraft (vertical/short take off and landing), the Navy's propensity to concentrate combat assets in rings around the carrier is incapable of meeting the Soviet submarine threat and needs to be replaced by an operational concept emphasizing stealth and dispersal. This requires a wholly different shipbuilding plan that would emphasize aircraft carriers suitable for antisubmarine warfare and of much smaller tonnage than the large-deck carrier (anywhere from 20,000 to 40,000 tons as opposed to the 90,000 tons of the *Nimitz*-class carrier); and a cancellation of the major escort ships now planned by the Navy (the CG-47 *Ticonderoga*-class cruiser and the DD-51 *Burke*-class destroyer). The procurement of the *Los Angeles*-class attack submarines ought to be supplemented by a less expensive set of diesel submarines, which are more effective than nuclear-powered vessels in the barrier operations for which they are most needed.[1]

2. The Air Force needs to abandon its self-image as an "independent arm" capable of achieving an independent decision in battle. Emphasizing, like the Army, an attrition style of warfare, and geared for missions (like deep interdiction) that would in all likelihood be far less relevant to the course of a NATO war than others (like close air support), the Air Force needs an overhaul in doctrine preparatory to a change in weapons and tactics. The sophisticated electronic capabilities built into Air Force aircraft are without significant military value. Incapable of distinguishing between friendly and enemy aircraft except visually (and thus at close range), Air Force pilots could not use their expensive radar-guided missiles in combat. Equally mistaken is the growing emphasis on precision-guided weaponry and capabilities for the long-range surveillance and acquisition of targets deep in the enemy rear.[2]

3. The U.S. Army is on the way to self-reform but still has a long way to go. Its doctrinal concept of the 1970s was based on a firepower/attrition style of warfare, which conceived of battle as a contest for a favorable "exchange ratio" on the model of the World War I battle of

---

ranging to be satisfactorily classified simply under the label of reform. Boyd is a retired Air Force pilot with a distinguished combat record, whose oral briefing, "Patterns of Conflict," is said to have had a far-reaching impact on the reformers. The principal writings of the reformers will be cited in the pages that follow. Their influence is indicated by the extensive coverage their critique has received in the national news magazines, daily newspapers, and journals of opinion, both left and right. See, for instance, "The Winds of Reform: Runaway Weapons Costs Prompt a New Look at Military Planning," *Time*, 7 March 1983; Charles Mohr, "Drop in U.S. Arms Spurs Debate on Military Policy," *New York Times*, 24 October 1982; Morton Kondracke, "Defense without Mirrors," *New Republic*, 24 January 1981. The editorial page of the *New York Times* weighs in every month or so with a piece along reform lines.

Verdun. That, happily, has been replaced by a maneuver style of warfare that stresses movement over fire, though there are grounds for questioning whether the doctrinal shift has been fully absorbed within the Army. The leadership of the Army has moved to reduce the extraordinary turbulence in combat units, which in the 1970s spawned poor morale and inefficient training, but its "tail-to-teeth" ratio is still excessively large, and its habit of rotating troops individually rather than as units is still mostly intact. The procurement program of the Army has been little affected by these other reforms, and it is deeply flawed. Fixed-wing aircraft are far superior to helicopters in the attack role, and the main reason the Army has placed such heavy emphasis on the procurement of attack helicopters like the Apache is because fixed-wing aircraft (like the A-10) are under the control of the Air Force—which doesn't want them! The Army has completely misunderstood the role infantry will play on the battlefield of the future, a misunderstanding reflected in the procurement of the Bradley infantry fighting vehicle. Some Army systems, like the deeply flawed DIVAD air defense gun, have been canceled, but the decision was not supported by the Army leadership and had to be made by the Secretary of Defense, who himself succumbed to outside pressure.[3]

4. The direction NATO has taken over the past decade, largely under American leadership, is seriously flawed. Though the Army's new fighting doctrine shows some drift toward a maneuver style of warfare, NATO as a whole still has a force structure that lacks sufficient operational reserves to contend with Soviet breakthrough operations, which in turn are virtually destined to succeed given the brittle character of the NATO forward-defense strategy. NATO, moreover, shows a distressing tendency to rely on high-technology weapons that do not work and are enormously expensive. "NATO's military problem," Steven Canby has argued, "is conceptually quite simple. NATO needs more divisions —two or three times more." The Deep Strike initiatives are only the latest example of the propensity to seek a technological fix that, by its excessive cost and diversion of resources from more profitable areas, actually worsens the prospects for successful defense and deterrence. The reformers have explored a variety of approaches to expanding the NATO force structure, the most interesting of which is a restructuring of reserve forces on the model of the Dutch Rechstreeks Instromend Mobilisable (RIM) system, which releases its conscripts as units with equipment that may be recalled together to active duty within fifteen months of deactivation—while the personal relationships that make them effective fighting units are still intact. With this system, Steven Canby has argued, the Europeans could double their ground combat

contribution to NATO with only a 15 percent increase in total defense budgets. If air and sea contributions were reduced instead, such changes would require no additional expenditures and "could be offset alliance wide . . . yielding nearly a threefold increase in divisions with no loss in relevant air and naval capabilities." Such a change, in Canby's view, does not depend "on U.S. ground forces, technological complexity, or standardization," and indeed many reformers have argued in favor of substantially reducing the American ground force commitment to NATO. The reformers hold out the prospect of changes that would allow for a partial or complete withdrawal of American ground forces from Europe and at the same time would provide NATO with "conventional superiority." "NATO would be able to mobilize and deploy more rapidly than the Soviet Union and therefore be able to threaten the crown jewel of the Soviet glacis, East Germany, with a counterattack."[4]

5. Current American capabilities of armed intervention, particularly (but not only) in the region of the Persian Gulf, are seriously deficient and must be improved, if necessary at the expense of our forward defense of Western Europe. The Rapid Deployment Force (RDF), Jeffrey Record has argued, suffers from inadequate strategic and tactical mobility and is critically dependent for its effectiveness on the cooperation of regimes in the area — cooperation that may not be forthcoming. A necessary, though perhaps not sufficient, condition for overcoming the deficiencies of the RDF lies in the creation of a sea-based intervention force with "forcible-entry" capabilities. This restyled RDF would be centered on a greatly enlarged Marine Corps, which in turn would have to transform itself from a largely infantry force to one equipped with an array of light armored vehicles and prepared to fight with a maneuver style of warfare.[5]

6. All the services have demonstrated a preference for high-technology "state of the art" weapons systems that budgetary realities make it impossible to procure in the necessary quantities. The result has been a force structure far inferior to one stressing less technologically complex weapons systems procured in greater numbers. In general, the reformers prefer the smaller and simpler weapons platform over the larger and more complex one, usually have more faith in the gun and heat-seeking missile than in the long-range radar-guided missile, and if forced to choose, prefer quantity over quality. Indeed, they go much further than most analysts in this matter, arguing that the cheaper weapons that can be built in greater quantity are often individually more effective in combat than the more expensive weapons that replace them.[6]

7. All the armed services save some elements of the Army and the Marines have become bureaucracies resistant to if not incapable of adapting to the novel requirements of warfare, as the American experience in Vietnam painfully illustrated. The number of general officers is grossly excessive in comparison with past experience and in relation to present need. This central fact has led to a host of adverse consequences, from the overstaffing of technical bureaus (which results in endless and detailed specifications that drive up weapons costs) to rotation policies that "punch tickets" but prevent the development of real expertise in either the operational or the staff commands. The military education system neglects the study of military history, which ought to be the true foundation of professional understanding, and indeed encourages the education of officers in every field save the one that is central to its raison d'être. The striking feature of the American military profession, in sum, is precisely its absence of professionalism.[7]

The foregoing summary represents a composite picture of the military reform movement, and it is not clear that any individual reformer would adhere to every element within it. Indeed, there are a number of striking disagreements within the reform movement on the larger questions of American strategy. The reformers disagree among themselves on whether the United States should have a primarily continental or maritime strategy — that is, on whether scarce resources should go into the land forces (ground and tactical air) or the Navy; on whether the United States should gear itself toward fighting the "long war" or the "short war"; and on the general attitude the United States should adopt toward interventions in the Third World — a question with important implications for the number and composition of forces designed for extra-European contingencies. These are not incidental matters; they involve the basic questions of national strategy.

These disagreements have led to some interesting, and unremarked, tensions within the reform movement, of which there appear to be four central areas:

1. The doctrinal and technological critique of the Army has as its principal implication an increase in force levels equipped to fight a rapid war of movement in Europe. Such an increase in force levels would in all probability require a return to conscription. At the same time, however, some reformers believe that the contribution the United States makes in ground forces to Europe's defense should be sharply reduced.[8]

2. The recommendation to reduce the size of American ground forces in NATO is inconsistent with the emphasis that the reformers of tactical air power place on close air support, for this mission (according to the

reformers' own writings) requires very close collaboration between air and ground commanders and hence must be related to the size of the contribution the United States makes to NATO's defense on the ground.[9]

3. The premise of the doctrinal and technological critique of the Army and the Air Force — that a war in Europe would more closely resemble the German blitzkriegs of 1939-41 than the positional warfare of World War I — assumes that the United States should focus on preparation for the short war, whereas the premise of the doctrinal and technological critique of the Navy is that the United States should gear its naval forces toward ensuring that the Russians could not interdict the critical sea lines of communication across the Atlantic, a posture that makes sense only on the assumption that we should place primary emphasis on the long war.[10]

4. The common emphasis on reforming the Marine Corps by increasing its capabilities for inland operations against Soviet-style armed forces in the Third World while still preserving its capacity for amphibious operations against hostile Third World opposition is incompatible with the strategic guidance to the Navy to focus on fighting the Soviet Navy. The former emphasis requires an increase in "power projection" capabilities, whereas it is precisely these capabilities that are deemed irrelevant to fighting the Soviet Navy.*

Given such far-reaching disagreements and tensions within the reform movement, it will no doubt appear puzzling that those associated with it should be held to constitute a movement at all. It would be misleading, however, to deduce from these disagreements that the reformers have grouped themselves together merely because "reform" is an attractive banner under which to congregate, and that they have nothing in common but a word. The reformers do constitute a "movement." They do so not by virtue of the positions they have taken on

---

* Cf. Hart, "Military Reform Budget," which recommends canceling the Navy's plan to "bring back the battleships" and suggests reducing the number of attack aircraft in the carrier air wing, with Record, *Rapid Deployment Force*, who proposes an increase in "forcible entry capabilities" and urges the return of the battleships. Most of the tensions within the reform movement stem from the fact that it is made up of a diverse group of independent thinkers who nevertheless share a number of themes. Yet the writings of individual reformers are not free of internal contradiction. Canby's views on the importance of close air support and his suggested reduction of the U.S. Army's role in Europe are one instance of this. Another is the argument of Fallows, in *National Defense*, that "it is dangerous to develop systems whose effectiveness depends on a specific set of circumstances." Fallows recommends that we "develop forces and strategies that give us the greatest possible capacity to adapt to whatever the future brings" (pp. xiv, xvi, 174). But this view is difficult to square with his condemnation of "gold-plating," since the

American strategy, but rather in their common critique of the American armed services' respective theories of warfare. Put differently, the consensus among the reformers exists on the issues that arise at the professional military level; their disagreements are on the strategic issues that involve political judgments (and that the theory of civil-military relations advanced earlier assigns to civilians). The military reformers constitute a movement because they all believe that the American services do not understand the character of contemporary warfare. From this misunderstanding, it is argued, flow most of the services' failures in doctrines, tactics, organization, and weapons systems.

Although centrally concerned with matters that go to the heart of the military's professional function, this critique has assumed an important place in the debate over contemporary military policy because it enjoys the support of civilians. Many present and former members of the services, it is true, have had a hand in formulating this critique, and it is apparent that in the past the reformers have often addressed themselves to a primarily military audience. But their views, which have been given a full airing within the military establishment, have not for the most part been well received, having had least success with the Navy and most with the Army, with minor inroads into the thinking of the Air Force and the Marine Corps. The reform movement is predominantly civilian in character in the sense that its effectiveness will come, if ever, as a consequence of reforms imposed on the services by the executive branch or the Congress. At present, the reformers enjoy their greatest strength in the Congress, where a bipartisan Military Reform Caucus has been established, yet reform ideas are not without weight in the executive branch, and there may come a time when they become paramount in the Office of the Secretary of Defense. But within the military services themselves — with minor exceptions — preponderant

---

tendency to over-design most often arises from the attempt to ensure workability in a variety of conditions and climates — from the hot, dry deserts of Arabia to the cold, wet plains of northern Europe, and from the conventional battlefield to one on which the possibility exists that nuclear, biological, or chemical weapons might be used against American forces. Moreover, his dismissal of the utility of the large-deck aircraft carrier and his argument that "there will probably be many more situations in which hundreds of smaller ships, or a larger, well-trained army, or a force of thousands of sturdy, reliable tanks would be more adaptable to our needs" is inconsistent with his emphasis on flexibility and unpredictability. The force he recommends is in fact useful in basically only one contingency: a large-scale conflict with the Soviet Union, and this is the least likely one we face. For the lesser (and unpredictable) uses of force that are necessary from time to time, the aircraft carrier is clearly superior to the mass force he recommends.

opinion in the respective officer corps is decidedly out of sympathy with most reform ideas and seems likely to remain so.[11]

Thus the peculiar character of the military reform movement. It is an attack on the existing set of military professionals that is waged in the name of military professionalism; and it has attained widespread prominence and support because it has been embraced by many individuals whose affiliation is with institutions that are preeminently civilian — the news media, the Congress, and to a lesser degree the academy. On the strategic and political issues where civilians must provide clear guidance to the military, the reform movement is divided; on the military issues where civilians are obliged (according to the theory of civil-military relations advanced earlier) to defer to professional judgment, the reformers are united and determined to effect change.

Positive Contributions and General Themes

Any assessment of the military reform movement must begin by noting the degree to which the reformers — almost single-handedly — reinvigorated the debate over military policy in the 1980s. Many of those associated with the reform movement — particularly Edward Luttwak and Jeffrey Record — have real literary talent, and reform themes have attracted the interest of journalists like James Fallows and Gregg Easterbrook, who are equally skilled with the pen. Whatever the overall merits of the reform critique, the reform movement as a whole did succeed in forcing into general public debate a set of issues that previously had been hidden away in the professional military journals, where as often as not they were treated in cursory and unsatisfactory fashion. At the least, then, the very breadth and originality of the reform critique has earned the reformers a place in the debate over American military policy comparable to that held by the limited-war theorists of the 1950s, the systems analysts of the 1960s, and the arms controllers of the 1970s.[12] Whether the reformers will ever enjoy the kind of practical influence that fell to these earlier movements remains to be seen; their place in the history of American military thought is in any case secure.

There is also little question that the reformers have made a positive contribution to the debate over military policy in a number of areas. They have urged that the study of military history be given a more prominent place in the military educational system — surely a worthy objective. And they have mounted a companion attack on the quantitative techniques and economic modes of (cost-benefit) analysis that McNamara brought to the Pentagon. They may have occasionally gone too far in this respect, for in some circumstances such analysis did yield interesting results. They were of value in assessing the merit of competing strategic nuclear weapons systems, allowing for the identification of "how much is enough" — though McNamara originally based that decision on quite traditional political and fiscal criteria.[13] And it was the Systems Analysis Office in DOD that observed — through quantitative analysis of the number, size, and intensity of combat engagements — that the Communists appeared to be capable of limiting their own casualties, an insight of profound significance in assessing the wisdom of Westmoreland's strategy of attrition.*

But the emphasis on quantitative skills, in Vietnam and elsewhere, also had results that were positively misleading and harmful. The harmful effects must be seen not primarily in terms of the effect on particular weapons systems but in the character of the inquiry this approach fostered and the misdirection of talent it led to. Instead of studying the history of warfare and deepening their understanding of combat effectiveness, too many military professionals came to specialize in the kind of knowledge their civilian supporters demanded, with consequences that on the whole were harmful. There is a strong tendency in quantitative studies to measure only what can be counted and to neglect the intangible judgments of strategic desirability and tactical effectiveness that are invariably of greater significance — the classic instance being the absurdly high kill ratios attributed to precision-guided missiles and duly emphasized in the models. Quantitative studies, it is true, can highlight the theoretical assumptions employed in constructing one's model, but the mass of studies employing such techniques normally do not do so, and in any case those assumptions are discoverable through quite normal processes of ratiocination. The attack the reformers waged on the application of such techniques to the study of military systems was therefore entirely justified. Those who have seen the limited results achieved by quantitative modeling in the fields of political science,

---

* See Lewy, *America in Vietnam*, pp. 82–84. It is one of the ironies of the war and of the quantitative methods associated with its conduct that the most notorious instance of the corruption induced by numerical measures — the "body count" — was itself exposed by quantitative techniques. The American commander most enamored of quantitative measures, Maj. Gen. Julian J. Ewell of the Ninth Infantry Division, set up quotas for his subordinates and "amassed an unsurpassed record of enemy casualties." But there is persuasive evidence, as CORDS observers put it at the time, "that the high body counts achieved by the 9th were not composed exclusively of active VC. The normal ratio of three or four enemy killed in action for every weapon captured was raised at times to fifty to one; this leads to the suspicion that many VC supporters, willing or unwilling, and innocent bystanders were also killed" (pp. 141–43). For a revealing example of McNamara's infatuation with quantitative measures, see Betts, *Statesmen, Soldiers, and Cold War Crises*, p. 186.

history, and even economics will not be surprised to learn that the results here were equally dubious.*

Equally beneficial has been the reformers' critique of the services' personnel policies. The rotation of officers and enlisted men at short intervals during the war in Vietnam did indeed, as the reformers have charged, have destructive results. This procedure exacted a terrible price in morale and contributed to the virtual disintegration of American forces by the end of that conflict. Turnover rates at the company level often ran close to 100 percent, and it is very nearly self-evident that the perpetuation of such turbulence for combat units — which require the mutual trust and confidence that can spring only from personal relationships — was certain to be fatal.[14] The Army in particular has attempted to overcome some of this personnel turbulence through the COHORT program, with results that are as yet uncertain, but the problem of inordinate rotation among general officers continues largely unabated. Much of this is due to the excessive number of general officers, for whom employment must be found. From 1945 to 1983 the number of officers at the rank of colonel/Navy captain and above has declined only slightly, from 17,057 to 15,455, whereas in the same period the total number of men and women on active duty has dropped from 12,123,455 to 2,127,422. The strategic rationale that supports this arrangement — preparation for a protracted conventional war with the

---

* The most interesting and wide-ranging analysis is Eliot A. Cohen, "Guessing Game: A Reappraisal of Systems Analysis," in Huntington, *Strategic Imperative*, pp. 163–91, though he too readily deprecates the value of the general procedure of comparing costs and benefits (employed by the economist) — which is quite similar to the reconciliation among political ends and military means in which the strategist engages. Both must revert to what Brodie calls "the conception of reasonable price" — "the idea that some ends or objectives are worth paying a good deal for and others are not" (*War and Politics*, p. 159). The possibility that the critics are beating "a horse that has been dead for fifteen years" is considered in Betts, "Conventional Strategy," p. 148. Stockfisch, *Models, Data, and War*, is a sharp indictment of "the data and models encountered in DOD-sponsored study and analysis," but Stockfisch concludes with the call for more analysis and believes that "it likely has not achieved its fullest potential" (p. iii). Modeling combat systems raises difficulties comparable to those encountered in modeling the economy, save that in combat there is no unit of exchange comparable to currency; and the assumption that there is can lead the analyst to place excessive weight on indexes of pure attrition, whereas in combat success or failure depends upon maintaining cohesive fighting units and disrupting the adversary's plans and morale (Cohen, "Guessing Game," p. 185). There is consequently every reason to believe that models of combat systems will prove far less useful than models of the economy; and the latter, as Lester Thurow has observed, have "not proven capable of providing either accurate forecasts or conclusively settling economic disputes." *Dangerous Currents: The State of Economics* (New York: Random House, 1983), p. 105 and chap. 4, passim.

Soviet Union — is not persuasive, if only because it is not consistently pursued elsewhere in the military establishment, whose munitions are barely sufficient for the first thirty days of such a conflict. And in peacetime, it has led to an overhead of disproportionate size and to paperwork of mind-boggling dimensions. There is consequently a good case for reducing the size of the officer corps — one that could be carried out alongside commensurate reductions in the civilian staffs of the Congress and the Office of the Secretary of Defense.*

The reformers have also placed deserved emphasis on adequately funding the budgetary accounts that are indispensable in maintaining readiness — which ought to be broadly defined to include not only funds for operational training and spare parts but also funds for manpower costs. The Spinney Report of 1979–80 was instrumental in drawing attention to critical weaknesses in the American forces' preparedness for war. That this case was made precisely at the moment when the external world suddenly darkened because of the seizure of the hostages in Iran and the Soviet invasion of Afghanistan made it very influential, and rightly so. The reformers, in addition, persuasively warned against the danger that the improvements made by the Reagan administration in this area would be short-lived if the administration refused to cancel some of the major weapons systems whose bills were coming due in the late 1980s. The reformers occasionally overestimated the cost overruns on weapons systems (based on a mistaken extrapolation from the experience of the inflation-ridden 1970s), and they often refused to heed either the role modernization plays in maintaining readiness or the extent to which extensive training (which they favor) might detract from readiness for war (because of extensive wear and tear on equipment). Still, the general imbalance they identified between the procurement accounts and everything else was real enough.[15]

---

* See Luttwak, *Pentagon and the Art of War*, pp. 18–21, 157–84. It is not clear that Luttwak has satisfactorily proved all the charges — some of them serious — he levels against the services' procurement commands; nevertheless, his insistence on the relation between excessive requirements in the design of weapons and the size of staff appears sound. The weapons prototype programs of the early 1970s sponsored by David Packard had small staffs, avoided detailed specifications, and encouraged the defense contractors to make trade-offs themselves — with results that were generally successful. See Smith et al., *Use of Prototypes in Weapon System Development*. If the services have a case for the overall size of their officer corps and their rotation policies, they have not made it. This is clearly an area where the services will have great difficulty in reforming themselves, and the case for civilian intervention here appears good. For an intriguing suggestion about how this might be done, see Gabriel, *Military Incompetence*, pp. 191–95.

Finally, the reformers have reminded us of the dangers of pursuing high-technology solutions to military problems. That there is a trade-off between quality and quantity is, of course, scarcely a new idea in military analysis. This was one of the principal themes of the whiz kids under McNamara. As Bernard Brodie has said of McNamara,

> It was not alone the lack of objectivity among the services concerning their respective needs that was at issue. It was his opinion that the individual services could not be depended upon to make wise decisions concerning their own major weapons systems. The record seemed to show (it would be difficult to argue the contrary) that they were too eager to expend large sums in the pursuit of some extra margins of speed or other characteristic of the performance concerning their ships, aircraft, or tanks — margins that might indeed have a tactical or strategic advantage but sometimes a very modest one that seemed to be hardly proportionate to the extra cost.[16]

The reformers succeeded in drawing renewed attention to quality-quantity problems in the late 1970s and early 1980s, and though they may have occasionally exaggerated their case in this field as well, many of their points are telling. The things that make a difference in combat, as the Israelis have so frequently demonstrated, are as often as not cheap modifications of existing equipment that require detailed attention to the tactical or operational situation rather than sweeping technological breakthroughs. Journalistic renditions of the quantity-quality theme have often gotten their facts a little confused (as in the trade-off some authors discovered between the F-15 and the A-10, planes designed for two entirely different missions), and the reformers themselves have occasionally played fast and loose with the financial statistics. More seriously, they have often written as if comparisons between flyaway costs for military systems are all that need be considered, whereas relevant comparisons must include total system costs (for additional personnel, fuel, spares, wartime bases, and training facilities). There is no gainsaying the point, however, that the malady they pointed to — extremely sophisticated weapons too expensive to procure and support in sufficient quantities (and indeed often canceled even before procurement) — was real enough.[17]

That there should exist, in the matter of quality versus quantity, this affinity between the military reform movement and the McNamara revolution is ironic, for (as noted) many of the reformers have little use for — and indeed have at times savagely criticized — the systems-analysis approach that in McNamara's hands was to rationalize the procurement of weaponry and the conduct of war. Nevertheless, the differences that exist between the military reformers and the intellectual perspectives that came to be known in their collectivity as the McNamara revolution should not obscure the deeper affinity between the two. The affinity lies not only in their common perception of the dangers of "gold plating" but also in the receptivity each of the movements found in the larger civilian world and their common hostility to the existing set of military professionals. Like many of the McNamara reforms, the program of the military reformers is based on the presumption of service incompetence. And as it was by McNamara, the doctrinal intransigence of certain elements within the services is viewed as the product of bureaucratic habit and not of professional understanding.

The Doctrinal Debate, NATO Reform, and Ground Forces

These positive contributions cannot be ignored in any assessment of the reform movement. Less convincing has been the stance the reformers have taken on doctrinal issues, in particular the way they have distinguished between two basic styles of warfare — attrition and maneuver. "Both doctrines," William Lind has noted, "employ fire and maneuver. However, in the attrition/firepower doctrine, maneuver is primarily for the purpose of bringing firepower to bear on the opponent to cause attrition. The objective of military action is the physical reduction of the opposing force." Attrition doctrine was held by the French army before World War II and was the basis of their disastrous defeat by Germany in the spring of 1940. It is "war in the administrative manner, of Eisenhower rather than Patton, in which the important command decisions are in fact logistic decisions. The enemy is treated as a mere inventory of targets and warfare is a matter of mustering superior resources to destroy his forces by sheer firepower and weight of material." It was until quite recently the doctrine of the American Army, enshrined in its basic operational field manual, FM 100-5 (a new edition of which was published in 1982 that borrowed heavily from the reform literature). Such a doctrine made a certain kind of sense, the reformers argue, when the United States enjoyed an overwhelming superiority in material, as we did in World War II. But the doctrine, it is argued, makes little sense against the Soviet Union, which holds a decisive advantage in most elements of combat power and indeed seems destined to retain such an advantage.[18]

The reform critique of the American style of warfare is thus an attack on "attrition doctrine." But the attack has two dimensions. The first makes the essentially strategic judgment that the methods of attrition are incompatible with a position of net material inferiority. On this view, an attrition style of warfare makes sense for the adversary with superior resources, a superiority that the North enjoyed over the South in the American Civil War and the coalition that destroyed German military power enjoyed in the two world wars. But a "fatal dissonance" has arisen when the side with a net inferiority in usable military resources continues to presume such superiority in its concept of operations. Its operational art is no longer consistent with its strategic requirements. This is the case today, the reformers argue, when one considers the respective positions of NATO and the Warsaw Pact nations on the Central Front in Europe.

The second dimension of the attack on attrition doctrine involves the operational judgment that NATO's cordonlike defenses are incompatible with armored warfare, and it differs from the other approach in critical respects. The assumption of the operational critique is that NATO would be incapable of making use of the war reserves — in both men and supplies — that it had accumulated, since the cohesion of its defense would be rapidly degraded in the first few days of a Warsaw Pact invasion. The strategic critique is much different. It holds that even without the vulnerability of NATO's cordonlike defenses there would exist a fatal dissonance between the methods of attrition and a position of net material inferiority. The reason seems obvious. Even if one assumes an "exchange ratio" that favors the defense, the side with greatly superior military resources will eventually win out.

Both these critiques raise troubling issues. Army doctrine in the 1970s did place too little emphasis on "the principles of avoidance (to side-step the major Soviet thrusts), deception (to mask the defenses), elusiveness (in small scale counterattacks) and momentum (on the counterstroke)." But it makes a big difference whether the reformers' concept of operations "involves mini-Cannae style operations which meet the attack up front, deliberately open a 'gate,' and then slice into his vulnerable flanks at the 'gate post'" (as Josef Joffe has described one interpretation of this strategy) or whether the reformers are arguing for either counterattacks deep in Eastern Europe or a series of strategic retreats. If the former is all that is involved, "it is not so much reform," as Joffe has observed, "as a gloss on contemporary *Bundeswehr* tactics in the service of the forward defense orthodoxy. If it is the latter, the Germans will not be flattered." For they will either be deeply disturbed by the sacrifice of territory the mobile defense strategy requires or appalled by the exponential increase in nuclear risks that a strategy of conventional retaliation would bring.[19]

It is not only that these proposals represent a political cul-de-sac (which the reformers are willing to concede). Militarily they are also questionable, and in any case the political and military issues cannot be separated as readily as the reformers would like. Indeed, it is likely that a strategy of "conventional retaliation" would deepen NATO's military predicament because it would exacerbate the vulnerability of the Alliance to surprise attack. That vulnerability arises not from the likely absence of sufficient warning indicators of Soviet preparations for war, but rather from the possibility that the will of Western statesmen would falter at a critical juncture for fear that countermobilization would, in the manner of 1914, make war inevitable. The vulnerability to surprise attack (and hence to disruption and organizational collapse) would therefore be increased by a strategy of conventional retaliation. If mobilization does occur on time, the forward-defense strategy offers a sound basis for a successful defense; and though it would certainly be desirable to have greater operational reserves to call upon, it is a bad military bargain to find such reserves by denuding those forces currently committed to forward positions.[20]

The strategic critique is equally misleading. A position of net material inferiority is not incompatible with a strategy of attrition. If we understand this term as it has traditionally been used — that is, as denoting a strategy that seeks to exhaust the enemy (as opposed to annihilating his forces in a decisive battle of maneuver) — it will become apparent that the reform critique has not been borne out in a range of historical cases. Indeed, the weaker parties to conflicts have frequently and consciously resorted to such an expedient to prevail over stronger opponents — the classic examples being Frederick the Great's conduct of the Seven Years' War (at least in its later phases), Washington's strategy in the American War of Independence (during which he successfully avoided the destruction of the Continental Army), and the conduct of the war in Vietnam by the North Vietnamese (during the American phase from 1965 to 1973). It is true that the historical record contains many cases of weaker parties attempting to compensate for their material inferiority through preemption, and it is of some interest that the two armies most admired by the reformers — the German and the Israeli — have often achieved their most striking victories in this manner. It would be foolish to deny that in some instances this recourse has paid striking dividends. But preemption is irrelevant for NATO, and in any case the historical record as a whole does not favor it. For both Germany and Japan in the twentieth century, the proclivity for the bold stroke either added to the number of their adversaries or increased the enemy's ferocity. There is, admittedly, dissonance between a position of net material inferiority and the strategy of attrition — in that the weaker party must always be concerned that the will of the stronger might prove indomitable. The dissonance, however, is not necessarily or inevitably fatal, and indeed the weaker party may ultimately invite its own destruction if it does not act from a true appreciation of its underlying weakness and vulnerability, as General Lee discovered at Gettysburg and as the Japanese found to their sorrow in the Pacific war.

We need not rely on historical cases to show the relevance of a strategy of attrition for NATO, for the critical vulnerability of Soviet strategy resides in the probability that the morale of the ordinary Soviet (or Eastern European) soldier would collapse if the divisions leading a Soviet invasion of Western Europe were destroyed — if NATO, in other words, were to prevail in the short war. If the forward defense of West Germany held and NATO's forces were overcome only after their supplies of ammunition and fuel were exhausted — if the Russians, in other words, faced the prospect of a grinding war of attrition in which their principal hope of victory lay in pulling the teeth of NATO power instead of a rapid war of maneuver in which NATO's capacity to deliver firepower was disrupted by severing the NATO tail — then in all likelihood the NATO conventional forces, though suffering from a net material inferiority and hence deficient in staying power, would provide the basis for an effective defense. The prospect of success would depend on essentially the same factor that determined the success of a strategy of attrition in the past: the disruption of the enemy's morale. The great instance in modern warfare of such a disruption through defensive operations is the complete collapse of discipline within the French army as a consequence of the Nivelle offensives in 1917, a crisis of which the Germans were fortuitously unaware and that was not overcome until the appointment of Pétain. If the NATO defense line holds in the first stages of a war, that is a danger that the Soviet Union can by no means discount.[21]

It is a measure of the complexity of these issues that many of the changes the reformers advocate in the NATO posture might be undertaken without any doctrinal revision at all. Though some of the structural changes (such as the sharp reduction of tail-to-teeth ratios, on the Soviet model) make sense only on the basis of a change in doctrine, others need to be considered primarily in terms of the improvements they might offer in the existing posture. This is particularly true of the proposals to increase the number of European ground divisions, a reform proposal that has gained widespread support among defense analysts.[22]

Proposals to add additional armored divisions to NATO often foster the impression that such increases in combat power would be virtually cost free, as in Canby's reflection that "the problem is not more money." That is not the case. Given the likelihood of stable (or even in some instances declining) European defense budgets in the latter half of the 1980s, these divisions, recently estimated to cost more than $97 billion over ten years, could be paid for only by eliminating some other feature of the balanced forces maintained by Britain, France, and West Germany. These three powers are the critical ones, for they have by far the largest reserves of manpower. Yet the air and sea forces of these three powers provide the Alliance with valuable auxiliaries that are duplicated nowhere else. It is fanciful to ask the Europeans to give up their air forces. Whatever the merits of the proposal from a military point of view — and no one has ever demonstrated that it would improve matters — it would appear wholly unattractive (and not only a little insulting) to the Europeans were the United States to make such a proposal. Every dictator worth his concessionary aid has an air force of sorts (sometimes even equipped with the latest American models). Why not the Europeans?

If we consider the interests of the West as a whole, moreover, there is little to be gained by denuding the Western European powers of their capacity to act in the extra-European world. The French checked Mu'ammar Gaddafi's ambitions in Chad (though admittedly not without some initial embarrassment to the Mitterand government). The British victory in the Falklands was a welcome tonic and would have been very difficult to achieve had the European orientation of British military forces been carried much further (as had indeed been planned). The implicit division of responsibility, whereby the Europeans would tend to regional matters and we would tend to their interests in the extra-European world, is a bad bargain for us and for them.

It might be argued that France and Britain could pay for such expanded ground formations by cutting back on plans to expand their nuclear forces, but this too is undesirable. The bargain, in effect, is that the Europeans should rely on the United States to a greater degree than they now do for their nuclear deterrent, and therefore a proposal that seemingly offers the promise of a more independent Europe in military affairs would in fact force them to deepen their dependence in precisely the area where such dependence is most resented.

The proposals of the military reformers, so far as they relate to Europe, thus raise a host of objections, quite apart from the changes that require doctrinal innovation. Insofar as military reform in Europe is simply a call for the Europeans to spend more resources on defense, the proposals are not particularly novel. Insofar as it represents an attempt to reorder Europe's balanced force structures within the confines imposed by stable defense budgets, the proposals are undesirable. Indeed they are worse, for they are strongly reminiscent of the patronizing attitude the United States adopted toward the French in the 1960s — which led France to withdraw from the NATO military command in 1966. If made a central feature of a new American initiative toward Europe, they would no doubt have equally unfortunate consequences.

The feature of the reform critique that has attracted most attention, at least in the Congress, concerns the Army's procurement program. The far-reaching character of this critique is perhaps best indicated by the alternative "military reform budget" that Gary Hart presented in 1984. The reform budget recommended canceling what the Army considers its most important initiative in aircraft: the Apache helicopter, together with its main armament, the Hellfire missile. As an alternative, it urged the development of a follow-on to the A-10 attack plane. Of the Army's two main initiatives in armored combat vehicles, the M-1 tank and the Bradley M-2 and M-3 infantry and cavalry fighting vehicles, the Hart budget favored eliminating the Bradley and procuring an ungraded M-113 APC. An earlier statement of the reform caucus called for extensive retesting of the M-1. The reform budget also called for halting the procurement of the Army's two main initiatives in air defense, the Division Air Defense Gun (DIVAD) and the Patriot missile, and recommended instead the development of a "family of passive radar-homing anti-aircraft missiles, to include a surface to air missile," the possible reintroduction of the "Duster" twin forty-millimeter self-propelled antiaircraft gun, and a "competition among existing towed, optically guided anti-aircraft guns." Apart from the M-1, it is no exaggeration to say that the reform budget struck at the heart of the Army's modernization program.[23]

The grounds of reform opposition to the Army's modernization program are various. The objection to the Bradley M-2/3 is at bottom to the whole concept of armored vehicles from which the infantry can fight, as opposed to personnel carriers — like the Bradley's predecessor, the M-113 — that are basically nothing more than armored taxis that carry infantry to the battlefield, where the infantrymen dismounted. The complaint against the Apache AH-64 is similar: at bottom the reformers do not believe in the utility of attack helicopters as tank killers. Not merely the Apache but all such attack helicopters — especially in a European environment — are "less effective and less survivable as an attack aircraft than a properly designed fixed-wing airplane." Whereas the reform opposition to infantry fighting vehicles and attack helicopters is rooted in doctrinal opposition, the ground of attack against the Patriot surface-to-air missile and the Division Air Defense Gun is somewhat different. Both the Patriot and the DIVAD are radar guided, and there is no theme more insistent in reform literature than that radar guided missiles are inherently defective. The high cost of the Patriot, the reform budget noted, when combined with its low kill probability, "makes it unlikely we can procure it in quantities sufficient to be meaningful." The DIVAD was also said to be "inherently flawed in its design, in that radar-guided anti-aircraft guns do not work well against maneuvering aircraft or helicopters hovering a few feet above the terrain."[24]

That parts of this critique were telling is indisputable. Secretary of Defense Weinberger canceled the DIVAD after a series of tests that the system failed spectacularly (and that seem to have been rigged by the Army's operational testing bureau). The Bradley appears to be equally defective, in that it was designed to operate with the M-1 tank, though the Army now acknowledges that such operations would expose the infantry fighting vehicle to such a concentrated array of Soviet antiarmor missiles that few commanders would be willing to use it in this fashion. Overdesigned if its function is to be simply an armored taxi and insufficiently protected if it must accompany main battle tanks, the Bradley is a classic instance of a military system that falls between two stools.

The reform critique of the attack helicopter is far less persuasive. All modern armies equipped for armored warfare envisage some role for the attack helicopter, including those two much favored by reformers, the German and the Israeli. Such systems, moreover, would play a central role in any Soviet operation against Western Europe (to say nothing of the effective use the Soviets have made of their Hind attack helicopter in Afghanistan). Although helicopters lack the range and payload of fixed-wing aircraft and therefore cannot concentrate firepower at widely separated points in a conflict, in more limited tactical situations helicopters organic to the ground forces might prove extremely effective. It is therefore fundamentally misleading to claim, as many have done, that the Army developed attack helicopters only because it could not, by an executive decree of 1957 (subsequently rescinded), procure fixed-wing aircraft of more than 5,000 pounds.[25] Fixed-wing and rotary aircraft complement one another in the close-support role, and it is only a narrow view of the problem of "duplication" that would force the services to procure one system to the exclusion of the other.[26]

Whatever the inadequacies of the Army's procurement program, there is something profoundly disturbing in the vitriolic attacks the reformers have made against the Army in this area. The central assumption underlying the entire reform critique is that the officer corps of the Army is professionally incompetent, that in the procurement of weaponry this corps has demonstrated a startling and altogether characteristic ineptitude, that it is precisely within the area of its professional function that it has most completely gone awry and is most in need of reform. Military reform, particularly in the Congress, has therefore come to be identified with the proposition that the Army cannot be trusted to develop its own weaponry and that Congress must exercise a detailed and minute supervision over it. On the other hand, one of the central themes of the military reformers is their celebration of "maneuver warfare," which must be understood in part as a call for allowing much greater initiative to the lower levels of command and which is therefore predicated on the assumption that the Army's officers are of a very high order of competence and that the lower levels of this officer corps may be depended upon to exercise their discretion wisely. There has been no attempt to reconcile these assumptions in the literature on military reform — for the very good reason, perhaps, that they are irreconcilable.

There are few themes more prominent in the literature on military reform than that the services have demonstrated a preference for high-technology "state of the art" weapons systems that budgetary realities make it impossible to procure in the necessary quantities. After a certain point, one the American armed services have long since passed, quality ceases to be a substitute for quantity. Yet it is on this very question — the appropriate size of the U.S. Army — that the reform position is most difficult to characterize. This is so for two reasons. One is that the reformers often couple their proposals for NATO reform with suggestions that the U.S. Army be partially or totally withdrawn from Europe; another is that the reform movement has become identified with a proposal to shift the responsibility for non-NATO land operations to the Marine Corps, with a (mechanized) Corps becoming, in effect, the nation's Rapid Deployment Force. Yet if considered together these two proposals clearly undercut the rationale for maintaining anything approaching a 780,000-person Army, for if this Army is not to be the primary instrument of American power in Europe and if it is to be eliminated from armed missions in the world beyond Europe, it is difficult to see what is left of its role. To the reform critique that has drawn most attention — that the Army's weapons would not work in combat against Soviet forces in Europe — must be added the strategic assumption that the reform of NATO's defensive posture rests primarily on European forces themselves, not on American ground forces.

Some of the reformers therefore urge us to increase the size of the Army, others, to reduce it.

One way of reconciling this apparent contradiction is through much greater reliance on reserves, fitted out with greater numbers of less expensive planes and tanks. Such a policy was proposed by the National Guard Association in its *VISTA 1999* report (drafted with the aid of some of the reformers) and is supported by a number of other critics not commonly identified with the reform movement.[27]

There is nothing wrong in principle with expanding the fighting capability and numerical strength of American reserve formations. They amount to a form of insurance in case another large-scale conflict on the order of World War II, Korea, or Vietnam occurs within the next ten years. Even in the latter two conflicts, "limited" though they were, American resources were taxed. In Korea the United States was forced to rely heavily on the reserve manpower that had fought in World War II, and in Vietnam it drew heavily on active forces stationed in Europe and the United States. As with most such decisions, however, such expanded reserve formations would not be cost-free. And if considered in relation to other parts of the U.S. force structure that would lose resources because of a decision to expand the reserves, the proposals appear much less attractive.

Reserve formations in the ground forces have, for one thing, traditionally maintained much lower levels of readiness than active forces. Although no doubt much could be done to raise the readiness levels of existing units, there is the danger that such units would still take a long time to mobilize and would be basically useless in the first stages of a Soviet-American war. Once ready, moreover, transporting such forces to an overseas theater would require greatly expanded airlift or sealift capabilities — an expensive proposition. Insofar as peacetime preparation is directed toward the possibility of a Soviet-American war, it makes little sense to undermine one's prospects for winning the short war in order to marginally improve one's prospects in the long one. Scarce resources, therefore, ought to be devoted to increasing the capability of NATO forces to prevail in the first stages of a conflict (by increasing ammunition reserves from thirty to sixty days and beyond, for instance) rather than by devoting resources to forces that in all probability could not be made ready for combat immediately. If, after the first two or three months of a war in Central Europe, NATO forces do not constitute a cohesive line but are instead broken remnants, there will be nothing for these reserve forces to reinforce. In those circumstances the attempt to regain a toehold in Europe would require years of mobilization, to which the prior efforts in the way of reserve forces would make only a minor contribution.

The most striking feature of these proposals to expand the reserves is how frequently they are coupled with proposals to reorient existing ground forces to threats to American interests in the Third World. Not all reformers are "interventionists," but there is a strain of thinking in the reform movement, represented best by Jeffrey Record, that is heavily so. Yet of all reform themes, those that call for reorienting American ground forces to the Third World are the least persuasive. The difficulty is not only that withdrawing American ground forces from Europe, either in part or in toto, might renew the security crisis in the Alliance. More important, the use of American ground forces on a large scale in the Third World is fundamentally inconsistent with the limited character of American interests in such areas; worse, the use of such forces affords prospective enemies the opportunity to strike us at our most vulnerable point — that is, our unwillingness to sustain large casualties.

The fundamental difficulty with reform interventionists such as Record is that they would apply the Nixon doctrine to Europe — where it is inapplicable — and abandon it for Third World contingencies, where it continues to be relevant. Yet it is in the Third World that the distinction the Nixon administration drew between ground forces, on the one hand (which were to be provided by our allies), and air and naval forces, on the other (which were to remain an important American responsibility), continues to express a sound balance between military power and political commitment. It splits the difference between isolationists and interventionists in as sensible a fashion as possible, for it makes clear that the United States has the military capability to impose a severe penalty — through either aerial attack or economic blockade — on states contemplating aggression against their neighbors, a fact that ought to have some influence on the calculations of such heavily armed states as North Korea, North Vietnam, Iran, Syria, Libya, Nicaragua, and Cuba. It makes it plain that primary responsibility for providing manpower must be taken by the threatened peoples themselves or by their allies in surrounding regions. And it is consistent with the outlook of the American people, who are averse not to the use of force as such, but only to force of a certain kind.[28]

If (as argued earlier) the reform distinction between attrition and maneuver tells us very little about our basic military and strategic choices in Central Europe, it is profoundly misleading when applied to the possibility of using American ground forces on a large scale in the Third World. It will not do to argue that maneuver warfare would mean low American casualties and an attrition style of war would mean higher ones. After all, the emphasis that American forces have traditionally placed on firepower has been due in large measure to their desire to expend machines rather than men. More fundamentally, the number of American casualties in such conflicts depends not on the style of warfare but on the scale of the ground-force commitment and the protracted character of the war. It is difficult to imagine the circumstances in which any one of the Third World states previously mentioned — all of whom are headed by resourceful leaders — would not be capable of imposing substantial casualties on American ground units and forcing a protracted commitment in the event of such an American intervention. For these reasons, the distinction between maneuver and attrition styles of war basically confuses the issues at stake in potential Third World interventions; it implicitly elevates the question of operational art to a higher status than the more fundamental problem of reconciling interest and power. That is a fundamental mistake in analysis. "War cannot be divorced from political life," Clausewitz observed, "and whenever this occurs in our thinking about war, the many links that connect the two elements are destroyed and we are left with something pointless and devoid of sense." All the tactical and operational brilliance in the world cannot make up for strategic error — else the Germans would now rule half the world and Ariel Sharon would be the king of Lebanon.[29]

THE FUTURE OF THE CARRIER TASK FORCE

The reform critique of the U.S. Navy involves a basic challenge to the Navy's most cherished tactical and doctrinal concepts, yet this critique should not be confused with an attack on naval power itself. Indeed, some of the reformers — particularly Gary Hart — are in favor of increasing the Navy's share of the military budget relative to those of the other services. Hart has called for a "maritime strategy," though the meaning he assigns the term is quite different from that given it by former Secretary of the Navy John Lehman. Such a strategy, in Hart's view, is indispensable for an "island nation" as dependent as the United States on overseas commerce for its "survival." "I am not fighting," Senator Hart says, "against the big aircraft carriers. I am fighting for more aircraft carriers."[30]

In 1982 the Reagan administration requested (and received) authorization for two *Nimitz*-class carriers in its fiscal year 1983 budget submission. It made the same request in 1987. The administration's carrier proposals lay at the heart of its plans to build a 600-ship navy centered on fifteen carrier battle groups. Yet the opposition of Hart and other reformers to the *Nimitz*-class carrier must be distinguished from that of those who opposed the authorization of the two carriers on the grounds that too many resources were being put into the Navy's budget and not enough into those of the other services. For Hart has shown great interest in procuring different kinds of carriers in much greater numbers.

In 1982 Hart recommended not only canceling the big carriers but also procuring an "alternative design aircraft carrier" of about 40,000 tons intended primarily for antisubmarine warfare and "capable of launching current as well as V/STOL aircraft and costing no more than one-third as much as a *Nimitz*-class carrier. Alternative carrier designs presented to the Senate Armed Services Committee" in 1982, Hart says, "included a ship with these characteristics." He proposed procuring one ship of this class each year. "Assuming a thirty year life for such a ship, a building rate of one ship annually will support a fleet of thirty carriers."[31]

In 1986 Hart proposed procuring a range of even lighter carriers — some as small as 8,000 tons — that would carry mostly V/STOL aircraft.[32] But though the details have differed, the guiding idea remains the same. The basis for this alternative ship-construction program is Hart's conviction that the "big carrier with its current airwing is largely irrelevant to fighting the Soviet navy, which is primarily a submarine navy." The "small versus large carrier analysis," Hart says, "does not address that issue." Instead, it "asserts the superiority of the large carrier versus the small carrier in abstract terms." The critical question for him is whether "a 15 carrier Navy, which increasingly dedicates its assets to the protection of the carrier," is "prepared to defeat head on a superior Soviet submarine fleet."[33]

The debate over the respective merits of the small- and large-deck aircraft carrier is not straightforward, if only because it involves a wide array of technical questions that are answered differently by each side. When political and strategic differences are added to this debate, as they necessarily are, the result is often perplexing. Perhaps the key difference between the reformers and the Navy is whether carriers considerably smaller than the 90,000-ton *Nimitz*-class or 80,000-ton *Forrestal*-class are capable of providing their own fighter protection. In part this debate turns on whether technological advances will allow vertical and short takeoff and landing (V/STOL) aircraft to achieve range and payload capabilities comparable to those of the high-performance aircraft that are today launched from the large-deck carriers. Many who believe that V/STOL aircraft can achieve much greater capabilities than they have today, such as Stansfield Turner, argue that "the day of the missile" is just beginning in aerial warfare and that the coming domination of air battlefields by the missile will render high-performance aircraft like the F-14 obsolete. The "F-14s successor could well be an aircraft with only modest speed and maneuverability, but a superior missile system. Such an aircraft could be on a carrier one-third the size of present carriers, and even smaller."[34] Others note that the British Aerospace Harrier can be configured as a superb dogfighter, one whose capabilities in this regard were clearly validated in the Falklands war. Even among the proponents of the V/STOL Support Ship (VSS), then, there are serious differences over the future character of naval warfare and the future direction of technology that would make the VSS both necessary and possible.

The contribution a VSS might make to the battle for air superiority is critical in determining its possible role in the fleet. If smaller carriers cannot provide their own fighter protection, then they need to be considered primarily as supplements to the existing carrier force, not as replacements.[35] If they are considered to be supplements, moreover, then their true competitors in the fleet cease to be the aircraft carriers and become instead, depending on the mission foreseen for the smaller carriers, a variety of other vessels. When the Navy proposed to bring the 40,000-ton *Oriskany* out of mothballs in 1981 — a proposal Congress turned aside — it was evident from the aircraft that would have been placed on this modified "Essex" carrier that its real competitor was the battleship. With a wing of Marine A-4 light attack aircraft, the principal function of such a carrier would have been to provide "flying artillery" support for the Marines, whereas the function of the battleship is to provide floating artillery. Such a carrier could form the center of a surface action group in peacetime, as the battleships do, but in war it would require the fighter protection provided by the large-deck carrier. A VSS configured for antisubmarine warfare, on the other hand, would have as its competitor an entirely different class of ships and aircraft — mainly the configuration of land-based patrol aircraft (P-3C Orion) and surface escorts (including the "low-mix" FFG-7 *Perry*-class frigate as well as other older frigates and destroyers in the fleet) now maintained by the Navy for antisubmarine warfare.

It is difficult to dispute the Navy's view that there is at this time no foreseeable replacement for the large-deck carrier in its role of providing sea-based fighter protection. Not only is the large-deck carrier capable of launching fighters with much better performance than existing V/STOL aircraft, but the technological developments that might allow for improvements in the range and time on station of V/STOL aircraft would allow for commensurate improvements in the capabilities of CTOL aircraft like the F-14. If it is true that "the age of the missile" is just beginning, it does not necessarily follow that the aircraft carrying such missiles need not be high-performance aircraft. The development of precision-guided missiles in enemy aircraft like the Backfire or the Blackjack may require carrier-based fighters to intercept at even greater distances than they now do. Aircraft that lack the performance to challenge attackers at standoff ranges are irrelevant in meeting this threat; so too are superior dogfighters like the Harrier and the F-18.

The advantages of the large-deck carrier do not end here. The better sea-keeping qualities of the larger carrier allow the launching and recovery of aircraft in sea states that would either prohibit or make very dangerous recovery operations onto the smaller carrier. This would be an operational factor of critical significance if enemy land-based aircraft were capable of getting airborne. Effective fighter operations, moreover, require a variety of early warning, reconnaissance, electronic warfare, and tanker aircraft. The number of such aircraft for effective operations tends to be fixed, leaving less room for the fighter and attack aircraft that are at the heart of the carrier's defensive and offensive capability. The smaller carrier, therefore — whether a 10,000–30,000-ton VSS or a 40,000–50,000-ton CVV capable of handling CTOL aircraft — would not only tend to degrade the defensive capabilities of the battle group by making operations in rough seas difficult if not impossible and by reducing the size of the outer defensive perimeter its fighter aircraft were capable of maintaining, but would also sharply reduce the battle group's offensive capability by forcing a reduction in the number of attack aircraft.

The second difference between the reformers and the Navy concerns whether the tactical configurations of the carrier battle group are basically sound. This configuration, as noted earlier, calls for a defense in depth. No longer, the reformers believe, is it capable of meeting the threat posed by the Soviet navy. Radar and sonar emitting strong signals to locate enemy targets, George Kuhn suggests,

> permit the enemy a distinct information advantage since he can detect our sensor and communications signals many hundreds, even thousands, of miles beyond the point where our sensors can pick his up. The problem is compounded by the fact that our fleets continue to use World War II tactics that place the high-value targets (the aircraft carriers) in the center of distinctive rings of protective escorts. The combination of active electronic emissions and old tactics gives the enemy the opportunity, before our fleet even knows he is there, to plan and execute intense attacks on our forces, which are arranged in veritable bull's-eye patterns.[36]

The current carrier battle group is thus inescapably vulnerable to mass Soviet attack, the critical contingency for which the Navy should be prepared, yet its naval shipbuilding program is devoted increasingly to the task of protecting the limited offensive power provided by the carrier air wing. The reformers believe the Navy should distribute its aircraft over a much larger number of platforms, which would ensure that the losses inevitable in naval warfare will not be catastrophic.[37]

There is indeed a problem with the Navy's program to procure the CG-47- and DD-51-class AEGIS escorts. But the central difficulty concerns not the technical matters that have most agitated the reformers — on which uncertainty abounds — but rather the budgetary resources the Navy would need to fulfill its stated plans — requirements that inevitably compete with those necessary to ensure the modernization of U.S. land and tactical air forces. The question, in other words, must be seen in the light of the long-standing debate between proponents of "continental" and "maritime" strategies.

If we imagine a war with the Soviet Union in Central Europe (where the Soviets maintain their largest concentration of combat power), it seems clear that the marginal advantages afforded by additional investments in naval forces would almost certainly be outweighed by programs designed to improve the readiness and staying power of U.S. ground and tactical air forces. Naval power in such a conflict would be of foremost utility in securing the use of the seas for the United States and denying such use to the Soviet Union. As such, it is of primary relevance in a protracted conflict, in that it is only over a considerable period that the Soviet Union might be made to feel the effects of sea denial; and only in a protracted conflict would we need the reinforcements to overseas theaters that sea control makes possible. That the command of the seas is a desirable strategic objective is therefore clear; the difficulty is that, given the limited character of American resources, funds devoted to this objective must be taken from forces that would be relevant in achieving some kind of decision in the first stage of a Soviet-American war — that is, from ground and tactical air forces. The heavy equipment necessary to support such forces can be prepositioned in Western Europe, to which troops can be ferried on mobilization in ordinary civilian aircraft. All other manner of stocks can also be prepositioned and protected, with the result that retaining the use of the seas is not indispensable in the first month of a conflict. For this reason, the heavy investments in naval forces supported both by the Reagan administration and by military reformers such as Hart appear to be a bad bargain: if NATO forces are routed in the first stages of a conflict, there will be no line for the United States to reinforce.

Two other factors are relevant in considering the significance of naval power in a protracted conflict with the Soviet Union. One is that, over time, the Soviet Union faces serious disadvantages in prohibiting (or at least making very costly) Western use of the seas, since its submarines must transit through narrow geographical choke points and are not well equipped for sustained operations. Over time, therefore, it is likely that a naval strategy making use of attack submarines, mined choke points, convoys, and land-based patrol aircraft could gradually win control of the seas even if a substantial number of aircraft carriers were lost in an initial Soviet salvo. Second, even if the carrier battle group were to survive the coordinated conventional torpedo and cruise-missile assaults that the Soviet navy is capable of launching against it in a surprise attack, its ability to survive a nuclear salvo is far more questionable. Because collateral damage would be minimized in a nuclear war at sea, the Navy has a special vulnerability here that even extremely expensive escorts would have difficulty guarding against.

If the discussion thus far seems heavily weighted in favor of a continental strategy, that is partly because of the case we have been considering — a large-scale conflict with the Soviet Union in Europe. But that, of course, is a partial and limited perspective: there is little reason for believing that the world is on the brink of a third world war. If we cast the net somewhat wider and consider the role naval power has played in maintaining American interests in the extra-European world, we will find that it has proved its worth on many occasions. A maritime strategy — with its associated instruments of aerial attack and naval blockade — is more appropriate if non-Soviet contingencies are considered, and these are far more likely than another conflict of the World War II variety. For these conflicts there is no real competitor to the large-deck aircraft carriers, which are capable of protracted deployments to distant oceans and have frequently proved their utility in dealing with threats to American interests from non-Soviet states. Against these lesser opponents, however, sophisticated air-defense systems such as those carried on the two AEGIS escorts are not necessary. And if we postulate a Soviet-American contingency, it is very doubtful that these systems would justify their cost in comparison with air and ground forces.

These considerations suggest that there is a good case for scaling back the procurement of the two AEGIS escorts. At the least, the budgetary crunch the deficit makes inevitable means that the Navy will face a choice between reducing the number of surface escorts it desires and reducing the number of deployable carriers in the fleet. But these considerations also suggest that the alternative shipbuilding program proposed by Hart and other reformers is defective on several counts. It would pour resources into naval forces at a time when a contrary budgetary emphasis is desirable. And it would disrupt still further the continuity and coherence of the Navy's shipbuilding plan and concept of operations at a time when the budgetary shortfall will have succeeded amply in throwing naval affairs into confusion.

THE CONTROVERSY OVER AIR POWER

The reform critique of the Air Force centers on three closely related points: the value of manned aircraft performing bombing missions deep in Warsaw Pact territory; the appropriate aircraft and operational techniques for fighting air-to-air battles with enemy aircraft; and the emphasis that should be placed on close air support and the appropriate design of close-support aircraft. If the reform critique was accepted, it would require a sweeping change in the tactics and technologies of the NATO air forces. Indeed, it would make obsolescent a large portion of the NATO investment in tactical air power resources.

The reform critique is based in the first instance on the contention that the deep penetration of Warsaw Pact territory by manned aircraft is becoming less useful. There would be two basic objectives of any such campaign against the Warsaw Pact — air base attack and deep interdiction — and neither is likely to be accomplished at a price worth paying. This is so, the reformers argue, for a number of reasons. Warsaw Pact airspace is dense with a sophisticated array of surface-to-air missiles, and these would probably exact a large price from NATO manned penetrating aircraft. Even if significant attrition was not imposed on an attacking NATO force, it would be extremely difficult for such a force to accomplish its objectives. The value of interdicting Pact supplies, the reformers argue, is particularly open to question.[38]

The cogency of this critique of the deep-penetration mission — especially in a conflict with the Warsaw Pact nations — was partially admitted by the Air Force in the 1970s. None of its major procurement programs in the 1970s — the F-15, F-16, and A-10 — was designed with the deep-interdiction mission principally in mind. The reasons for this departure from the criteria that had traditionally shaped the procurement preferences of the Tactical Air Command was stated clearly by James Schlesinger in his fiscal year 1976 report to Congress:

> As the cost of procuring and operating tactical aircraft has risen, the Air Force has tended to select multi-purpose aircraft optimized more toward pursuing the air superiority battle and the interdiction campaign than toward close air

support and shallow interdiction. The result has been the long-range, heavy fighters of recent vintage. Now, however, several conditions dictate, not a reversal of this trend, but a shift in emphasis. As we have seen from the last war in the Middle East, sheltered aircraft are extremely difficult to destroy. And where concentrated air defenses are present, they can exact a heavy toll of attacking aircraft. There is also the problem in Eastern Europe that the network for railroads and roads is sufficiently dense so that a deep interdiction campaign, even with Precision Guided Munitions (PGM's), would take considerable time to work its impact on the fighting front, and probably could not prevent a considerable leakage of tonnage to the forward edge of the battle area (FEBA). In a war of surprise and rapid movement, these effects might well occur too late to break the momentum of an enemy assault.[39]

This was the basic justification for the Air Force procurement programs of the 1970s. As a consequence of it, the aircraft suitable for the deep-interdiction role had dwindled by the end of the decade. In the early 1980s the Air Force sought to reverse this trend. It now plans to procure up to 400 aircraft that are suitable for deep-strike missions. A competition between derivatives of the two main Air Force fighters — the F-15E and the F-16E — was held in 1983 to determine which plane would fulfill this role, and in 1984 the F-15E was selected. The renewed emphasis on the manned bomber was revealed not only in Air Force plans for the F-15E, but also in its resurrection of the B-1B bomber (suitable for some conventional roles) and the consideration it gave to proceeding with the F-16E (a plan subsequently abandoned owing to budgetary pressures).

This renewed emphasis on the manned bomber was widely greeted as an instance of the ruinous consequences that would inevitably follow from the Reagan administration's decentralized approach to defense management. The services, on this view, simply brought out all the old "wish lists" that were central to their "organizational essence."[40] But the evident implication — that the case for the manned bomber was threadbare — was misplaced. For one thing, the long-range bomber would likely prove to be of particular utility in contending with a Soviet attack on the Persian Gulf through Iran, whose deep gorges and narrow mountain passes are ideal for an interdiction campaign. The limited number of basing facilities in the region — even if "access" is granted — puts a premium on quality over quantity. The location of these bases also puts a premium on range, which is partly a reflection of the emphasis on "high performance" in aircraft like the F-15 and the F-111 much criticized by the reformers.

Even in Central Europe the case for the manned bomber is impressive. The threat to enemy air bases and choke points (such as bridges and railway stations) ought to be maintained in some fashion, for it greatly complicates Soviet war planning, forces a diversion of resources into defensive systems, and makes it plain that a war of conquest on their part will not be confined to Central Europe. That interdiction failed in Vietnam — often stressed by the reformers — is basically irrelevant to an assessment of its potential significance in Central Europe. Soviet operations depend upon maintaining the initiative and hence the continuous movement of second- and third-echelon forces onto the battlefield. The threatened disruption of this movement is a significant military objective. And though it may be that a force of long-range ballistic missiles would be a more cost-effective way of conducting an air campaign against interdiction targets and air bases, the political obstacles to placing such a force in Europe are formidable, especially in the aftermath of the campaign for the Pershing IIs.

Even if we accept, for the sake of argument, that the case for the manned bomber is weak in Central Europe, its potential utility in the Persian Gulf still argues for a significant deployment of such long-range systems. It is not only in the Gulf, however, that such a force could prove useful. The long-range bomber has a variety of maritime applications (with, at times, significant advantages over naval forces: a fleet of long-range bombers could have interdicted the movement of Argentinian forces to the Falklands at the outset of the conflict, whereas a reliance on naval power alone forced Great Britain to accept a temporary loss of the islands). Indeed, a force of long-range conventionally armed strategic bombers could constitute the main element of our global strategic reserve and Rapid Deployment Force. If procured with aerial radar capable of identifying moving and stationary targets at long range and armed with precision-guided air-to-surface missiles that can lay down all manner of improved conventional munitions, it could constitute a formidable strategic force against a wide range of potentially hostile states.

The differences between the reform movement and the Air Force over the appropriate design of tactical aircraft configured for air-to-air combat have perhaps stirred the most controversy. Two of the reformers, John Boyd and Pierre Sprey, were closely involved in the development of the F-16, initially procured as a daylight air-superiority fighter with excellent capabilities for aerial dogfighting. Though additional weight was added to the aircraft, which increased its attack capabilities, the F-16 A/B retained a recognizable likeness to its prototype. The further changes in the F-16 that the Air Force proposed, as part of the Multinational Staged Improvement Program (MSIP), will allow the F-16 to incorporate a new radar-guided missile (AMRAAM: Advanced

Medium Range Air-to-Air Missile) as well as the night and all-weather attack capabilities provided by the LANTIRN and IRR Maverick programs. None of these projected "improvements," the reformers have argued, would work as advertised. "The best way to 'enhance' the F-16's capabilities," Gary Hart has argued, "is to leave it alone."[41]

The reform case rests upon the following considerations. First, they maintain that radar-guided missiles beyond visual range have consistently demonstrated poor combat performance. Because such radar-guided missiles are heavier and have usually required a sophisticated and heavy avionics package in the missile-carrying aircraft, reliance on them has increased aircraft size and weight. The consequence, in every Air Force fighter program until the development of the F-16, was aircraft ill suited to the requirements of combat. These aircraft, such as the F-4 Phantom (originally developed for the Navy but ultimately adopted by the Air Force in large numbers) and the F-15 Eagle, represented improvements over their predecessors in certain categories—like top speed—but these qualities are irrelevant to their effectiveness in battle. Cruising speed is far more significant than top speed in enhancing surprise, the critical element in 80 percent of fighter kills. The sophisticated avionics and radar capabilities carried by aircraft like the F-15, moreover, act as a beacon alerting enemy combat aircraft to one's presence and fail to serve any useful purpose. The intelligence thus provided cannot be made use of by the firing of radar-guided missiles, because such missiles have not solved the IFF (identification, friend or foe) problem. Consequently, the rules of engagement in a European conflict are likely to demand visual identification, as they did in Vietnam. A European conflict would be a confused melee in which hundreds of combatant aircraft would be so intermingled that visual identification would be absolutely essential if downing friendly aircraft was to be avoided.[42]

Clearly, the reformers contributed much to the debate over tactical air forces, and on balance their influence has been positive. The development of the F-16 in the early 1970s was a real success story, one that probably would have been derailed had civilians not thrown their support behind the "fighter mafia." But the further development of the plane by the Air Force, which provided it with attack capabilities, was also a reasonable choice (though scorned by the reformers). The fighter mafia, moreover, succeeded in lessening the overall weight of the F-15, in a manner that has improved its probable operational performance. The reformers have also warned persuasively against stressing high-technology solutions (such as those increasing top speed) that are difficult to justify by their operational value. And they have drawn much-needed attention to the necessity of ensuring that the Air Force has sufficient war stocks to actually prosecute a conflict. Munitions that are so expensive they can be procured only in limited quantities and would be exhausted in the first few days of a large-scale conflict are a questionable bargain. And though the Air Force plausibly argues that the readiness crisis at the end of the 1970s was due to a decade-long underfunding of the readiness accounts, nevertheless budgetary constraints are something the Air Force must take account of in its force planning and weapons development. It is doubtful, for instance, that the extremely sophisticated capabilities built into the LANTIRN system, which would allow pilots to discriminate between tracked and wheeled vehicles and which have been largely responsible for its escalating costs, are worth the price.[43]

If the reformers have made a good case for the low-cost fighter and for adequately funding the readiness accounts, they have been unwilling to concede the operational utility of the sophisticated electronic and command and control capabilities reflected in the F-15 and the Airborne Warning and Control System (AWACS). The use the Israelis made in Lebanon of "aerial radars and jam-resistant communications tied into computerized command and control facilities" suggests, as W. Seth Carus has argued, that these are "essential features of modern air combat." The reformers have too readily depreciated what Walter Kross calls "situational awareness" — the ability to initiate air battles beyond visual range, which the Israelis did in Lebanon and which is central to U.S. war-fighting concepts. "What looks confused to the inexperienced analyst," Kross added, "may be the very environment where masterful air leadership is decisive." The reformer's concept of the air battle relies upon a limited number of combat-proven missions (particularly aerial dogfighting in clear weather) to the exclusion of a range of other missions (like operations in poor weather or at night). The force structure they recommend leaves serious gaps for the Soviet planner to exploit and would allow him to "conceptually outmaneuver the Reformers' limited warfighting construct."[44]

A third area of controversy — one related to the disputes over the appropriate means of maintaining air superiority and the utility of interdiction or air-base attacks by manned penetrating aircraft — concerns the relative emphasis that should be placed on the mission of close air support and the kind of planes that should be procured to fulfill it. The Air Force's traditional preference for high-performance multimission aircraft gave it a force structure ill equipped for the war in Vietnam, and in the first years of the war the Air Force was forced to use the propeller-driven A-1E for close support. The recognition of these inadequacies led first to the procurement of the Navy's A-7 and then to the development of the A-10 close-support plane. Most analysts agree that this plane, designed around an internally mounted thirty-millimeter cannon, would be an effective tank killer and is well equipped to assist in inflicting severe punishment on a Warsaw Pact armored thrust against NATO.[45]

There do exist differences between the Air Force and the reformers over the appropriate design for a close-support plane, with their points of view amounting — on this as on other issues — to conflicting appraisals of the utility of the missile and the gun. But the most significant difference concerns not the design of close-support aircraft but the emphasis that is to be placed on this mission itself. The basic Air Force contention is not that close-support aircraft like the A-10 are not extremely effective in certain circumstances, but rather that such aircraft cannot create the conditions under which they will be effective. Air superiority is, in the Air Force view, the necessary condition of effective close air support. The Air Force therefore contends that it is better to acquire aircraft like the F-16, which can be used effectively in the initial battles to gain air superiority but are also capable of converting later to the close-support role, than specialized close-support aircraft like the A-10. Its development program therefore calls for procuring the thirty-millimeter gun pod that can be attached to F-16s and used in the close-support role. The reform contention that the F-16 configured for the ground attack mission will be less effective than the A-10 thus does not really address the basic Air Force position, the key to which is that air superiority must be established before extensive air assets are devoted to close support.

A consideration that tells greatly in favor of the Air Force position is the constraint on forward basing in Europe that exists for American tactical air power. Of the five wings outfitted with A-10s, only one (108 aircraft) is based in Europe in peacetime. Since the reform case rests so heavily on the importance of bringing tactical air power to bear in the close-support role early in the battle — before the battle for air superiority has been won — it seems that the limited resources available for close support would be better distributed by ensuring that existing A-10s were capable of exerting a significant effect on the early days of a NATO war rather than by procuring additional aircraft that would be incapable of deploying rapidly to Europe in a crisis.[46]

MILITARY REFORM AND CIVIL-MILITARY RELATIONS

The foregoing analysis of the military reform movement supports two broad conclusions: one is that a great many of the changes in force posture and military doctrine recommended by the reformers are undesirable from a strategic point of view; the second is that most of the changes they call for at the professional military level are questionable at the least. Many of the reform themes are plausible, to be sure, and a few are compelling. But if we consider the reform program as a whole it is clear that the reformers have not met the burden of proof we ought to require of civilians who seek to force far-reaching changes on the military in matters that concern its professional function. In many of the instances we have examined, indeed, the services appear to have the better of the argument (and might be capable of meeting a heavy burden of proof if one were imposed on them). This is particularly so for the argument over American air and naval forces, which centers on the utility of the manned bomber and the large-deck carrier.

This failure brings into play again the many reasons for being wary of a civilian attempt to reform the military on the grounds urged by the military reformers. That the reformers' political strength is centered in the Congress is cause enough for alarm. The difficulty is not that Congress is filled with members who lack civic virtue and are indifferent to the public interest. It is rather that the nature of the institution is such that congressmen must serve first and foremost the voters in their own states and districts. It is no accident that the Military Reform Caucus has no coherent program and that the objectives of the inner group of military reformers have not been embraced by the caucus as such. The very character of the institution prohibits congressmen from consistently pursuing a course of action requiring adherence to anything so ethereal as a theory of warfare, and this is precisely what the program of the reformers demands. What Congress does best — representing and reconciling competing interests — necessarily involves it in making military policy. But to encourage its involvement not in the articulation of broad policy but in the details of weapons systems and tactics — as the program of the reformers inevitably does — would reinforce many of the worst habits that afflict defense decision making today.

Even if the program of the military reformers was embraced by some future Secretary of Defense, he too would inevitably face a set of powerful institutional obstacles. There is the potential for a crisis in civil-military relations even more far-reaching than the one that arose in the 1960s. The very comprehensiveness of the reform critique would make it difficult for a Secretary of Defense to play one service off against the others. Sensitive to the assault on their professionalism, in all likelihood the services would bitterly resent such civilian intervention and would rally round one another to resist it; in all likelihood, too, they could count on some powerful allies in the Congress. The services, moreover, would still have to be relied upon to implement a program that had been conceived elsewhere and to which they were hostile. Whether they would do so in good faith may be questioned.

Finally, it is apparent that implementing the reform program would require, at least initially, an extraordinary degree of centralization, with all its attendant liabilities. This is an inevitable feature of a comprehensive reform program imposed on the services from the outside. One may argue, to be sure, that the civilian intervention need take place only once, after which it would wither away, like the state. This, presumably, is the point of William Lind's contention that the "most fundamental long-term goal" of the civilian wing of the reform movement is to make reform "a continuing, self-generating process *inside* the services." "A successful civilian reformer is, ultimately, one who has made his own efforts irrelevant."[47] That is certainly a welcome goal; equally welcome is Lind's observation that "a reformed American military is not one that takes the ideas of the current reform movement and builds a rigid new structure upon them, but one that develops within itself an enduring capability for imaginative change, for self-renewal." Still, the habit of civilian intervention, once acquired, might not be easily broken, especially if the "self-renewal" of the services took a direction contrary to that desired by the reformers themselves. That has happened before, the most striking recent example being the failure of Elmo Zumwalt (Chief of Naval Operations from 1970 to 1974) to have much enduring impact on the Navy — an example that is particularly relevant given Zumwalt's receptiveness to many reform concepts.[48]

The military reformers have not written widely on the problem of civil-military relations, for reasons that remain unclear. They have subjected every other topic in American military policy to searching examination and comprehensive critique, and thus their relative silence on the issues considered in the first part of this book is curious. Yet it would not be unfair to infer from their writings that the reformers would accept the argument presented earlier that civilians must meet a significant burden of proof when seeking to impose far-reaching changes on the military in matters that concern its professional function. For the reformers are all believers in the idea of military professionalism — indeed, there are no more ardent defenders of the concept. That is what distinguishes the military reform movement from earlier civilian reform movements in American history, many of which were fundamentally suspicious of military institutions and "the military mind." It is speculative to say so, but their implicit recognition of the need for meeting a heavy burden of proof may account for the sweeping and intemperate character of the attack on the existing set of military professionals. That it has been both sweeping and intemperate is clear. The reformers have sought to show something more than merely mistakes in judgment by the American military; the American officer corps, in their view, has been guilty of "gross incompetence." The military has not merely committed errors; rather, it has displayed a pattern of "persistent professional malpractice that in any other profession would constitute grounds for disbarment, denial of tenure, or legal action."[49]

That case has not been made, though not for want of trying. The attempt to make it, however, has had one very serious consequence — causing the strategic prospects of the United States to appear far worse than they are. It is partly to the military reformers that we owe the perception that the Soviet Union enjoys overwhelming military superiority in Europe; and it is the military reformers who have managed to convert the liberation of Grenada into a humiliation for American arms. Neither perception is sound. The former rests on the view that everything would go right for the Soviet military and everything wrong for us; the latter would have us judge military operations by a kind of aesthetic standard — the brilliance of the American military's operational art — rather than by the only test that matters: whether the military fulfilled the political objectives the civilian authorities had set for it. On the latter, more important score, the operation was a success, and even from the standpoint of operational art it was not nearly as bad as the reformers have maintained. When given clear and attainable political objectives — as it was in Grenada but not in Vietnam or Lebanon — the military has performed reasonably well. There is room for improvement; there always is. But in our search for ways to improve military capability and operational performance, the most profitable area of inquiry is not the weapons systems and doctrinal proclivities of the individual services — which hold up reasonably well on examination — but rather the maladies inherent in our higher defense organization that spring from the lack of unified direction on both sides of the civil-military divide.

5 · The Question of Institutional Reform

In the postwar era, the United States has never lacked proposals for reforming the institutions that govern civil-military relations. Until recently, virtually all reforms had been successfully resisted. In 1986, however, Congress passed a Defense Reorganization Act that incorporated many of the proposals of the organizational reformers. Although it is still too early to say how the reforms will work out in practice, the Goldwater-Nichols bill was a substantial accomplishment. As might have been expected, Congress made far greater headway in reforming the Joint Chiefs of Staff than in changing its own internal procedures — many of which have had a deleterious effect on how efficiently the Pentagon is managed. Still, the changes made in 1986 were for the most part for the better, and it is not clear that the impulse toward organizational reform has been fully spent. The present moment, indeed, recalls the situation at the end of the 1950s, when a consensus existed among many Republican and Democratic leaders on the need for change, which yielded, in turn, the Eisenhower reforms of 1958 and the McNamara revolution of the early 1960s.

The debate on institutional reform in the 1980s was touched off by the comments of a retiring chairman of the Joint Chiefs of Staff, David Jones, who complained of several defects in the institution he supervised. It was given added force by the equally pointed criticism of military institutions that came from Gen. Edward C. Meyer, retiring Army Chief of Staff, whose critique was similar to that of General Jones, but whose remedies differed. Two independent civilian institutions — the Heritage Foundation and Georgetown's Center for Strategic and International Studies — produced reports in 1985 calling for widespread organizational change, and both of the Armed Services committees in Congress were active in holding hearings on the adequacy of existing institutional arrangements. Senators Barry Goldwater and Sam Nunn lent their bipartisan voices to the cause of organizational change, holding extensive hearings during 1985 and 1986. As the majority and minority leaders of the Senate Armed Services Committee, they publicized the results of a report on defense organization prepared by committee staff, whose conclusions in turn closely paralleled the argument of Samuel P. Huntington's widely read and closely reasoned essay "Defense Organization and Military Strategy" in *The Public Interest*. The President's Blue Ribbon Commission on Defense Management, chaired by David Packard, gave further support to the institutional reformers and was perhaps the main factor in overcoming the opposition of the Reagan administration to anything but minor changes in existing practices (most of which, the administration once insisted, could be brought about by executive decree).[1]

Much of what follows will be concerned with assessing the reforms adopted in 1986, particularly the changes that elevated the position of the unified commanders in relation to the service chiefs and strengthened the chairman of the Joint Chiefs of Staff, who will now have much greater power over the Joint Staff that serves the JCS. But because the Defense Reorganization Act did not do all it might have done, and because many institutional reforms are still on the table, it is necessary to cast the net somewhat wider and consider the proposals of the institutional reformers in their full diversity. Three other topics, in particular, deserve attention — those calling for:

— a reform of budgetary procedures that would induce more stability in the acquisition of weapons systems;

— a reorganization of the Department of Defense that would give greater authority to those holding offices concerned with the purposes the department must fulfill (strategic deterrence, NATO defense, and extra-European contingencies) and less weight to the functional areas (e.g., manpower policy) that support these functions; and

— a revision of the 1948 Key West accord, which allocated roles and missions among the individual services in a fashion that (according to the critics) has led to a host of deformities in force posture.

Many of these proposals for change are sound and deserve adoption: there is much in our current institutional arrangements that is subversive of an appropriate pattern of civil-military relations. Yet there has been a tendency in the contemporary debate over organizational reform to attribute certain ills to organizational defects when the real failure has been the more normal one of political intelligence. For this reason, many of the institutional remedies are unlikely to achieve the result their authors aim for and indeed may result in unintended (and undesirable) consequences. Others reflect a desire to change aspects of the defense decision making process that are deeply rooted in the character of our political institutions — which, whatever their deficiencies, are unlikely to undergo far-reaching change. The benefits that may be expected from the organizational change that is politically possible are almost without exception modest ones. Still, that is no reason to reject them. Marginal benefits are benefits nonetheless.

The Defense Budget Process

Of all the reforms that have been proposed to improve existing practices, those that call for change in the defense budget process are the least exceptionable. The deepening involvement of Congress in the micromanagement of the military establishment has made much more difficult the long-range planning that forms an indispensable part of both military effectiveness and administrative efficiency. The intrusion of narrow political considerations, to be sure, is not confined to the legislative branch. The decision made by the Carter administration to refit the aircraft carrier *Saratoga* at the Philadelphia Naval Shipyard (though it lacked the facilities to do a proper job) and, more recently, the bidding war that John Lehman conducted among coastal cities for the home porting of a newly refurbished fleet of battleships recall the observation of Mr. Dooley that "the first qualification of a Secretary of the navy was that he should never have seen salt water outside of a pork barrel."[2] Still, the propensity to view military policy in relation to narrow political needs is deeper in the Congress. Its division into two houses that have different perspectives on military systems, moreover, inevitably leaves a great many matters up for negotiation (and therefore subject to uncertainty) until the defense bill emerges from conference committee — in recent years invariably after the fiscal year has begun. Many of the most serious deformities are ineradicable features of American government and stem from the American Founding, the political equivalent of the Creation. Despite this fact, though, there are features of the existing defense budget process that might be changed given sufficient political will and that would represent a genuine improvement over existing practices.

One is the adoption of biennial budgets, whereby authorizations and appropriations would cover two-year periods instead of one year, as now. Such a change would allow each new Congress a full year to authorize and appropriate the military budget and to concentrate on a range of broader policy issues during its second session. The advantages of multiyear procurement would thus be extended to the whole of the defense budget. Biennial budgets would also have a salutary effect on planning and budgeting within the Department of Defense. Though modified in some degree, current procedures still owe a great deal to the PPBS ("Planning, Programming, Budgeting System") that McNamara introduced in the early 1960s. Annual budgets make the planning phase for future fiscal years overlap with the program and budget phase of the present year and the implementation phase of the past one. By itself, the adoption of biennial budgets would ease the confusion induced by overlapping schedules, and it would reduce the number of occasions when decisions already made were reexamined and refought.

A second change, though far more difficult to implement, would rationalize the congressional committee system by reducing the number of committees with jurisdiction over the defense budget. A variety of proposals have been put forward to accomplish this goal, including the reduction (from three to two in each house) of the committees (Budget, Armed Services, and Appropriations) with primary and overlapping jurisdiction over the defense budget; renewed emphasis on the distinction between the authorizing and appropriations committees (which would strip the Armed Services committees of their detailed power of annual review over line items); and a consolidation of the annual hearings each committee now conducts (which would ease the excessive burden on executive officials and staff, who now have to suffer endless pilgrimages to Capitol Hill to answer questions they have answered many times before). Of these, the third would not appreciably change the reality of the budget process and is in the category of proposals to be considered only if all else fails; the second would be difficult to enforce upon the Armed Services committees and would probably involve just as much political pain as the first set of proposals, which represent the best approach to the problem. The distinction between the authorizing and appropriations committees has lost its justification so far as the defense budget is concerned. The two committees in each house have increasingly come to duplicate each other's functions, and the additional layer of review adds nothing to the process but delay and more opportunities for obstruction. The most desirable reform would be the complete elimination of the appropriations committees and the transfer of their functions to the Budget, Armed Services, and Government Operations committees, each of which is necessary if Congress is to have a mechanism for enforcing fiscal discipline on the Pentagon, considering the broader issues of defense policy and military strategy, and reviewing the procedures by which the Pentagon procures its supplies.[3]

Others have called for even more sweeping changes. Jacob Stockfisch, for instance, has proposed that Congress and the Office of the

Secretary of Defense surrender their detailed review over line items. Stockfisch argues that the current system, whereby the military services attempt to justify their budgets in minute detail before skeptical civilians in both branches, leads to a whole series of information pathologies. As it now stands, the services have little incentive to review their own requests with detachment, since the resources lost through the cancellation of an unworkable weapon (like the DIVAD) cannot be applied to other purposes. A revised budgetary system, according to Stockfisch, would provide the military with budgets aggregated along mission and service lines: the services would enjoy the freedom "to make tradeoffs among the diverse, highly specific resources currently identified as budgetary line-items." Civilian supervision would remain, but it would be focused on the most important priorities among missions and services, each with its distinctive strategic implications. In conjunction with the unified operating commanders, moreover, civilian political authorities "periodically could evaluate the output of the military departments" through imaginative measures such as "readiness evaluation (including unannounced drills) that emphasize target location and identification, performance of reconnaissance missions, ability to carry out tactical and strategic deployments with limited advance notice, [and] capability to sustain operational activity."[4]

Theoretically, the advantages of such a system would be substantial. It would encourage civilians in both branches of the government to think in strategic categories and thus to fulfill their own peculiar responsibilities in military policy. It would do much to eliminate the intrusion of narrow political considerations (who gets what, when, where, and how) into the determination of military policy (which is why it will be resisted by the politicians). It would return responsibility and authority to the military services in a manner consistent with the level and scope of their professional expertise. It would discourage the development of costly technical improvements of dubious combat advantage, allow for flexibility in the use of resources, and substantially decrease the time between assessing need and providing troops with new combat systems (by eliminating several layers of review). Of all institutional reforms, it seemingly would do most to provide our system of civil-military relations with a form of objective civilian control.

Yet the practical difficulties of implementing such a system would be insuperable. Overlapping responsibilities between civilians and the military are a fact of life, and separating them through changes in budgetary procedure would be likely to raise a host of unforeseen problems. It is not clear, moreover, how the president and the Congress, lacking detailed control over line items, would express their inevitable disagreements over military policy (many of which involve strategic judgments and fall within their competing areas of responsibility). Finally, and most important, the reform would require a wrenching change in American political institutions. Even if the practical difficulties were overcome, the probability that the concept will one day be adopted by both branches is the same as for the prospect that fish will learn to whistle. Appearances suggest that they might; experience suggests otherwise.

Elevating Purposive Organization

According to many observers, contemporary American defense lacks purposive organization. There is a gap, in Samuel P. Huntington's words, "between strategic purpose and organizational structure." In the postwar era, the gap has existed on both sides of the civil-military divide. There are no civilian officials in the Pentagon with responsibility for the principal missions the armed services must carry out. There is, however, an army of assistant secretaries with responsibilities in functional areas like manpower policy and health affairs. The weakness of the unified commanders in relation to the chiefs of the military services, partly overcome by the Defense Reorganization Act of 1986, produced in the past a comparable effect on the military side.[5]

Organizational reforms that elevated purposive offices over functional (or supporting) groupings would, according to the critics, greatly increase the efficiency with which the Department of Defense conducts its business. On the civilian side, it has been suggested, the Defense Department needs three new offices at the under-secretary level responsible for the three major missions the armed forces must carry out (strategic deterrence, the defense of Europe, and force projection). On the military side, the change has already been effected with the strengthening of the unified commanders in relation to the service secretaries. By such arrangements, "the under-secretaries clearly would compete with each other for resources to perform their missions. Unlike current interservice competition, however, where only service interests are at stake, this competition would involve critical issues of priority among central strategic missions." Strengthening the authority of the unified commanders in relation to that of the service chiefs, on the other hand, would redress the current imbalance between modernization and readiness.

Most of these changes would probably represent a modest improvement over existing arrangements, but it is important not to exaggerate their significance. As the organizational reformers rightly observe, there is no civilian official in the Department of Defense with sole responsibility for strategic deterrence. On the other hand, decisions regarding strategic nuclear systems are usually not made by the Department of Defense. The Secretary of State and the National Security Adviser — along with their subordinates — will more often than not take a deep interest in these matters, and for this reason decisions on such matters inevitably — and rightly — will be made at the highest levels of the government. An Under Secretary for Strategic Deterrence might be better able to coordinate matters within DOD; on the issues that really matter, however, he will be merely one actor among many, and it is not obvious that he deserves a higher position than the Assistant Secretary of State for European Affairs or the head of the State Department's Bureau of Politico-Military Affairs, with whom he is likely to be in frequent competition. The same issues arise with respect to the proposals for creating under secretaries for North Atlantic and European Defense and for Regional Defense and Force Projection. As a practical matter, the most significant problems of coordination and direction are not internal to Pentagon organization but on the contrary involve matters that deeply affect the purposes of the other executive departments and the interests of allied countries. The purpose of the reform is to focus responsibility; the result would be to elevate somewhat the bureaucratic clout of one actor in what will continue to be a messy and confused process.[6]

Providing greater power to the unified commanders in relation to the service chiefs is a better idea, though its significance has also been exaggerated. All other things being equal, it is true that commanders responsible for operations in a particular theater will be more likely than the chiefs of the military services to favor expenditures for things like ammunition stocks, training, fuel, and other items that contribute to the readiness of existing forces, while the chiefs of the services will tend to be more concerned with the long term — with research and development, the modernization of weaponry, and the protection of force structure. But the critique of past arrangements is misleading insofar as it assumes that the reasons for the serious underfunding of readiness in the 1970s and 1980s are to be found in this institutional deformation. The United States faced a crisis in the late 1970s, as it will in all likelihood face one in the early 1990s, that involved a lack of readiness and sustainability. But the crisis in the first instance arose not because of organizational defects but because the Carter administration badly underfunded the force structure that it had, largely because it did not take seriously the problem of Soviet military power until forced to do so by the crisis that rocked the administration in the last year of its term. The Reagan administration's readiness crisis is of a much different character, but it too has a largely political basis. When setting out its program at the beginning of the 1980s, the Reagan administration made certain assumptions as to the overall growth of the defense budget — assumptions that were in turn based on very optimistic economic assumptions, which have not been realized. This error, combined with the administration's persistent refusal to cut out any major weapons systems procurements, has already created a serious crunch that will probably persist for some time. But there is no reason to place the blame for this state of affairs on a supposed imbalance between service and joint interests in the matter of readiness. The real reason is political, and the real failure has been one not of institutional deformation but of civilian judgment.

Increasing the authority of the unified commanders in relation to that of the service chiefs, incorporated in the 1986 reforms, was nevertheless a good idea. The act gave the unified commanders greater authority over the component commands, and it provided them with a readiness budget to cover the in-theater costs of the combat commands. The first change represents a substantial improvement over past arrangements, which gave the unified commander nominal authority over component commands that nevertheless remained heavily subject to the influence of the services. (With the encouragement of William Crowe, chairman of the Joint Chiefs of Staff, the Reagan administration had already moved toward this objective.) The second change has permitted each unified commander more flexibility in allocating resources in a fashion consistent with his responsibility for operations in a particular theater. The overall determination of the balance between readiness and modernization will remain a civilian responsibility, for the issue involves a range of political problems: an estimate of the immediate likelihood of war and a projection of the resources likely to be available for defense in the future, both of which involve matters beyond the level of military expertise. Still, such a readiness budget, as William Lynn and Barry Posen have argued, will "provide an institutional role in the programming and budgeting processes for the major constituency for readiness and sustainability concerns" and will enable civilian leaders "to make better informed judgments regarding the proper balance between longer-term considerations of force structure and shorter-term considerations of readiness and sustainability."[7]

Rewriting the Key West Accord

Another instance of the gap between strategic purpose and organizational structure often cited by Pentagon critics arises from the division of roles and missions agreed upon between Secretary of Defense James Forrestal and the chiefs of the individual services at Key West in 1948. Though modified in some details over the years, the division of responsibility arrived at then as a means of abating interservice rivalry remains largely intact. The Key West agreement, as Morton and David Halperin have recently noted, represented a compromise between the objectives of the Navy (which had urged that each service be given all the forces needed to carry out its missions independently) and the Army and the Air Force (who believed such a move would create unnecessary duplication). The Navy succeeded in retaining the Marine Corps; it also kept

> the authority to provide close air support for Marine land operations; and the authority to carry out those air operations, including ground-launched missions, which are required for sea battles. The Army and the Air Force, convinced that the services should avoid excessive duplication, were willing to give the Navy control over almost all sea operations. And the Army and Air Force agreed to cooperate with each other as a team on joint missions. Specifically, this meant that the Air Force pledged to provide the Army with airlift and close air support.[8]

According to the critics, the deformities this division of labor has caused are severe. Though the Air Force has responsibility for close air support and tactical airlift, it has been decidedly reluctant over the years to procure aircraft suitable for either mission, and this unwillingness in turn drove the Army to develop helicopters that are radically inferior to fixed-wing aircraft for both missions. The Air Force's responsibility for land-based ballistic missiles made it unwilling to consider an alternative mode of basing the MX missile (in submarines located in shallow coastal waters) that was far superior to the "solution" ultimately arrived at — placing the MX in vulnerable fixed silos. Finally, the Air Force's responsibility for airlift and the Navy's responsibility for sealift, neither of which is central to the "organizational essence" of either service and which the Army is forbidden to provide for itself, has left the United States critically short of strategic mobility assets. In each case, the Halperins argue, the institutional division of labor agreed upon at Key West has led to irrational decisions. Reform requires that

> no branch of the military should have to rely on other branches in order to carry out its duties. The Air Force would be given the responsibility for

strategic delivery of nuclear and conventional warheads from land, air, or sea. The Army would retain responsibility for large-scale ground combat but would gain the right to provide its own tactical airlift and close air support. The Navy would be responsible for control of the seas and have the right to buy whatever it needed, including unlimited land-based aircraft, to fulfill its duties. Its Marines would be responsible for all limited applications of conventional force, including ground operations launched from carriers.[9]

Neither the diagnosis offered nor the remedy proposed is sound. The indictment of Key West, to be sure, makes eminent sense on theoretical grounds; but the bill of particulars is another matter. In each case there are strong reasons for doubting that the Key West division of roles and missions was of primary importance in securing the results condemned by the Halperins. Two of their examples have already been examined. The evident implication of the critique is that the United States would have no helicopters for the missions of close air support or tactical airlift were it not for the "Key West key," but that assumption will not bear scrutiny. It leaves unexplained why the Soviets, the Germans, the British, the French, and the Israelis all envisage some role for the helicopter in both areas. Nor is it plausible to blame the supposedly inadequate state of American airlift and sealift capabilities on the Key West division of roles and missions. The Halperins write as if Vietnam had never happened and as if the anti-interventionary views it gave rise to among the public were of no consequence in determining the state of rapid-mobility systems in the 1960s and 1970s. In fact, however, reservations about intervention, even among conservatives like Richard Russell, were critical in killing both the C-5 and the FDLS (the Fast Deployment Logistics Ship). When those reservations began to be put aside in the late 1970s and early 1980s, largely because of the crisis in the Persian Gulf, the Key West accord did not prevent the Reagan administration from deciding to procure both the SL-7 fast sealift ship and the C-5B strategic airlifter (the latter over the objections of the Army Chief of Staff, who preferred to wait for the C-17). The central reason for the state of mobility systems in the late 1970s, in reality, was that civilians in the Pentagon, beginning with James Schlesinger and continuing through Harold Brown, focused on both the European Central Front and the necessities of the "short war," and that in turn led naturally to the choice of prepositioning over both airlift and sealift. Whatever the merits of these decisions, they were based on rational criteria and did not stem from institutional deformity.

The same appears to be true for the rejection of the SUM (Shallow Underwater Missile) concept. This was one of many basing modes considered for the MX, and its rejection first by the Brown Pentagon and then by Weinberger was based preeminently on a political unwillingness to move to a strategic force posture based only on land-based bomber and sea-based missile forces (the dyad). The land-based missile has special technical characteristics (reliability of communications, rapid retargeting) that were of central importance in the initial justification for the MX. Attempts to communicate with the proposed submarine force through "tie-in" systems would fix the force to an identifiable location and thus simplify the Soviet attack problem. The cost figures that the SUM proponents initially adduced did not include the antisubmarine warfare capabilities that would have to be dedicated to such a force, capable of patrolling a much smaller area of the ocean than the Polaris or Trident submarines. Nor was the submarine on which the initial proposal was based — the German HDW-600 — judged sufficiently survivable. The alternatives considered, however, drove up the cost to a level comparable to that of the land-based MX.[10]

Why the Reagan administration ultimately settled on a plan to place the MX in fixed (albeit superhardened) silos is a long — and admittedly strange — story. The unwillingness to tear up the states of Nevada and Utah, where Reagan had close political ties, was probably the determining factor in the rejection of the Carter MX plan; the subsequent rejection of "dense pack" and the political difficulties associated with other land-based options, combined with the administration's growing interest in strategic defenses (which placed the whole problem of land-based missile vulnerability in a different light), pushed it toward the package it ultimately embraced. It is certain that neither the Air Force nor the Navy thought the SUM concept desirable from its own point of view, but had the Brown Pentagon considered it superior on technical, political, and doctrinal grounds, there is every reason to think that it would have forced the concept on the two services, just as the McNamara Pentagon had done (though in somewhat different circumstances) with the Polaris submarine and the ballistic missile. The same appears to be true of the Reagan administration, despite its decentralized approach to defense management. The administration's strategic nuclear policy in general and the MX program in particular, to be sure, can be faulted on many grounds, but the men who crafted this policy did have a case for what they were doing. They wanted a land-based missile with hard-target counterforce capabilities, they ascribed enormous significance to the Soviet Union's force of such missiles (centered on the SS-18), and they believed that acquiring such a force was more important than solving the vulnerability problem. The policy can be faulted on many grounds, but in the end it cannot be attributed to institutional deformity.

If the emphasis on the Key West accord reflects a mistaken diagnosis, it is not surprising that the remedy also leaves something to be desired. There is no division of responsibility among the services that would achieve the result the Halperins aim for—a situation in which no branch of the military relies "on other branches to carry out its duties." The Army depends upon the Air Force to assure air superiority and on the Navy to provide sea control, and though these missions are central to the purpose of each service, there is no guarantee that the internal deliberations of the individual services, each with its new responsibilities, would be consistent with one another. The Navy might emphasize force projection over sea control, making the Army's sealift vulnerable in the first stages of a European war. The criteria each service employs in making such decisions would still require outside supervision and review, as now.

Reallocating all these roles and missions, finally, would cause great disruption, and not only of the retrograde bureaucratic kind. The training, outlook, and operational skill that makes for competent submariners is not something that can be produced overnight, especially among men who dream of aerial dogfights and daring bomber operations. No doubt the Air Force could learn to operate all those Trident and Polaris submarines (to say nothing of hunter-killer submarines armed with cruise missiles and therefore capable of "strategic delivery of nuclear and conventional warheads"); still, the proposal can appear attractive only to those for whom military organizations are lifeless entities whose operational skill is taken for granted and that are devoid of spirit, tradition, and loyalty.

JCS Reform

The institutional reform that drew most attention in the 1980s concerned proposals to change the Joint Chiefs of Staff, which in turn came in two main varieties. One set of proposals, largely incorporated in the 1986 Defense Reorganization Act, sought to strengthen the existing set of joint institutions. Building on the changes considered earlier, which strengthened the unified commanders in relation to the service chiefs, the moderate reformers in the Congress made the chairman of the Joint Chiefs of Staff the principal military advisor to the president, the Secretary of Defense, and the National Security Council. As the principal military adviser, the chairman now has the authority to offer cross-service advice without obtaining the approval of the other service chiefs, though each of the service chiefs retains the right to make his views known to the relevant officials in the executive branch and to the

Congress. The Joint Staff that currently serves the corporate JCS has become the chairman's own, and the military personnel system has been modified so that officers are "attracted, trained for, and rewarded for service in joint positions."[11]

Others have called for seemingly more radical reforms, in particular the institution of a Defense General Staff that would be separate from the four services, though drawn from them. Under such a system, which has been described in greatest detail by Edward Luttwak, "Army, Navy, Marine Corps, and Air Force officers of middle-high rank (say colonel/Navy captain) who have already filled staff and command positions and who have been selected for early promotion by their own service would be given the opportunity to start a new career as national-defense officers." Trained and educated "in the new format of national rather than one-service operations," such officers would be slated for staff and command positions "at a higher and higher level, over larger and larger groups of multiservice forces." The unified and specified commands would all be headed by senior national defense officers, "with their more junior counterparts in charge of the usual staff departments of each command. Even more senior national defense officers would be in charge of the main departments of a new National Defense Staff, at the apex of the entire military structure, whose task would be to provide professional military advice to the Secretary of Defense and the President, as the Joint Chiefs organization is now supposed to do." In the two-track system envisaged by Luttwak, "officers who chose to remain within their own service could still have a fully satisfying career reaching up to the highest ranks — except that if they remained one-service officers, they could not aspire to the higher direction of the armed forces." Lower-level commands would still be drawn from each of the services: "It goes without saying that warships should be commanded by sailors, divisions by soldiers, and air wings by airmen rather than by national defense officers who may or may not have originated in the relevant services." But the operational commanders of forces in an entire theater would be drawn from the new corps of national defense officers.[12]

The difference between these two sets of proposals is one of degree, not kind. Although Congress insisted that "the Joint Staff shall not operate or be organized as an overall Armed Forces General Staff and shall have no executive authority" (sec. 155 [e]), the prohibition serves primarily to ensure that civilian authorities retain control over the chain of command. The "joint speciality" that Congress instituted in each of the four services is intended to create a corps of officers familiar with the "forces, tactics, doctrine, jargon, and procedures" of all the services — as the proponents of a Defense General Staff demanded. If the new arrangements function as intended, they should be capable of ensuring that in wartime these forces are able to participate in coordinated operations and work effectively with one another. The commanders of both the unified and specified commands must have the joint speciality and must have served in at least one joint-duty assignment as a general or flag officer (sec. 164), and though the requirement may be waived by the Secretary of Defense, the congressional intent is to ensure that one-service officers cannot aspire to the higher direction of the armed forces. The effectiveness of the joint system, to be sure, will depend upon the support of the Secretary of Defense and the civilian heads of the military departments, but that is true of a Defense General Staff as well.

The most persuasive argument on behalf of these changes is that they will improve the planning and conduct of military operations. What Eisenhower said in 1958 when he called for the creation of the unified commands continues to hold true: "Separate ground, sea, and air warfare is gone forever. If ever again we should be involved in war, we will fight it in all elements, with all Services, as one single concentrated effort." As a prediction, Eisenhower's view of the future was off the mark, as the history of American combat operations in the past three decades makes clear. Yet he was right in thinking that "peacetime preparatory and organizational activity must conform to the necessity of unified direction."[13] Under the arrangements that prevailed until 1986, that was not the case. The difficulty was not merely that the component commanders, each beholden to his own service, had a disproportionate amount of influence within the unified command structure, but that the officers who were to direct unified operations (and the staff maintained to support them) had little sustained training in the exercise of joint responsibilities. The incompatibility of Army and Marine Corps radios, which prevented the separate ground force commanders on Grenada from communicating with one another, and the planning for the Iranian hostage mission, which involved throwing together units from all the services, each with its own procedures and in some cases even its own commanders, were only two instances of a malady that was deeply embedded in the previous system. The Joint Staff, which was supposed to cultivate such cross-service expertise, did a bad job in doing so, for the officers who composed it were expected to promote the interests of their own services.

This situation had to change, and the reforms effected in 1986 represent a promising beginning. The reform does not entail abolishing the individual services or diluting the special expertise that inheres in them. After all, the reformed Joint Staff will be composed of officers who have already distinguished themselves within their individual services and who will bring to the staff their varied and particular experiences. The 1986 legislation appears to recognize that while pluralism is a virtue in national strategy, it is a vice in the planning and conduct of military operations. Once the decision to use force has been made, and after all the compromises among the diverse strategic capabilities of the individual services have been effected, the paramount objective should be to ensure that the conduct of operations is truly unified and that the command structure has clear lines of responsibility. And though it is important to emphasize that the new arrangements will not necessarily work out in practice as Congress intended, they do provide the basis for a welcome improvement in cross-service expertise in the conduct of operations.

The most serious potential difficulty with the 1986 reforms — a problem that afflicts the proposals for a Defense General Staff as well — lies in the expectations that many observers have come to entertain for the role of the JCS chairman. The language of the congressional bill is careful to ensure that the chairman remains subject to civilian control. His duties include "assisting the President and the Secretary of Defense in providing for the strategic direction of the armed forces" and "preparing strategic plans which conform with resource levels projected by the Secretary of Defense." He will also be expected to advise the Secretary of Defense "on the priorities of the requirements identified by the commanders of the unified and specified combatant commands" and "on the extent to which the military program recommendations and budget proposals of the military departments and other components of the Department of Defense for a fiscal year conform with the priorities established in strategic plans." He must submit "alternative program recommendations and budget proposals, within projected resource levels and guidance provided by the Secretary," and must recommend "a budget proposal for activities of each unified and specified combatant command." Finally, he will be expected to recommend "changes in the assignment of functions (or roles and missions) to the armed forces," taking into account (among other matters) "changes in the nature of the threats faced by the United States; unnecessary duplication of effort among the armed forces; and changes in technology that can be applied effectively to warfare."[14]

The main danger of these directives is that they invite the military resolution of quandaries that are properly reserved for the determination of civilians. The military lacks the criteria — which are preeminently political in character — to decide the key questions of American strategy. A sensible resolution of the trade-off between modernization and readiness, for instance, requires a judgment about the likelihood of war in the immediate future, and that is a civilian responsibility. Choosing among the priorities of the various unified and specified commands requires an assessment of interest, and that too is a responsibility that belongs to statesmen. So also is the question of the priority of maintaining the sea-lanes (in a long war) as opposed to concentrating our limited military assets in forward positions (so as better to win, and deter, the short one). The professional military, to be sure, must always be free to object that civilians are asking them to perform impossible tasks with the limited resources available: the military commander, as Clausewitz observed, "is entitled to require that the trend and designs of policy shall not be inconsistent with" the means made available to him. "That, of course, is no small demand; but however much it may affect political aims in a given case, it will never do more than modify them. The political object is the goal, war is the means of reaching it, and means can never be considered in isolation from their purpose."[15]

There are, to be sure, many criticisms of JCS reform that exaggerate the dangers of the political role the chairman and his staff might play under the new arrangements. Some have argued that these arrangements will cause a reversion to strategic monism, but in fact no one knows what kind of strategy the chairman of the JCS would come to have were he expected to form one. Others warn of the "Prussianization" of American military institutions, but the analogy is in many instances misplaced, since the German General Staff was exclusively an Army staff and came to be completely dominated by the civilian Nazis in the course of World War II.[16] Still, the danger that the chairman and his Joint Staff would form their own political viewpoint — especially if they were encouraged to do so — does exist. With a couple of striking exceptions, the advice of the American military on the use of force in the postwar era has been quite sensible and usually no worse than that given by civilians;[17] nevertheless, it is fundamentally inconsistent with the central principle of civil-military relations for the military to intrude on matters of high policy, even if, as is likely, it were to do so with some reluctance. The appropriate determination of military policy inevitably involves some mixing or "fusion" of military and political roles, and any ordering of higher defense organization has to accommodate itself to that reality. It must also preserve, however, the more fundamental principle of civilian direction and military subordination.

The great object in the design of higher defense organization should be to ensure a plurality of military advice on those questions that involve an intermingling of political and military responsibilities — so as to preserve the ability of the president and the Congress to choose among them — and to ensure unified command and coordinated action on operational matters, which are primarily military in character. The reform of the JCS enacted by Congress in 1986 is by and large compatible with these objectives. The reform offers the prospect of a much-needed improvement in cross-service operational expertise, and the primary value of the changes lies in this area. On strategic and budgetary matters, the chiefs of the individual services are free to file dissenting reports, and the chairman of the JCS is unlikely to acquire too much political power unless the administration in power abandons its own responsibility to provide clear strategic direction to the armed forces.

The final point is the essential one. The chairman of the JCS should not be asked to proffer advice on the basic problems of American strategy. With the cross-service expertise now available to him, he might be able to identify unnecessary duplication among the services, and he might be able to suggest different ways of structuring the roles and missions of the individual services. On a range of military matters that touch the interests of the individual services, he will be well positioned to provide disinterested military judgments. But the larger dilemmas of national strategy involve responsibilities that civilian leaders must address, and we delude ourselves if we come to believe there is some kind of insight inhering in military expertise that is capable of resolving them and thus overcoming the American strategic predicament.

THE MODEST VIRTUES OF INSTITUTIONAL REFORM

Most of the institutional reforms that have been considered in this chapter have been around for a long time. In general, they address the feature of American civil-military relations that is least conducive to objective civilian control — the lack of unified direction on both sides of the civil-military divide. This lack of unity is deeply embedded in the American governing system: on the one side it stems from the separation of powers between the president and the Congress; on the other, from the existence of separate military services. The reforms that would be most effective in overcoming the lack of unified direction, however, are usually difficult to bring about and sometimes are of questionable desirability. Congress is most unlikely to surrender its detailed review over line items: were it to do so it would also surrender its power of distributing the loot among its varied constituencies. But it would also lose much of its power as a check on the excesses of both the executive branch and the military. It is very difficult to deprive Congress of the power to make mischief without simultaneously reducing its power to do good. Reforms that combat the lack of unified direction on the military side have proved themselves much more of a practical possibility, but not all are desirable. The extensive reallocation of roles and missions of the services would probably make matters worse. Even the reform of the JCS accomplished in 1986, though it offers the prospect of a much-needed improvement in the conduct of operations, will probably yield only modest benefits. Interservice rivalry has never lost us a war; nor has it ever prevented us from winning one. Institutional reforms are no substitute for sensible political and strategic choices, and it is a mistake to believe that they are.

The current wave of proposals for institutional reform therefore seems likely to issue only in the most modest of improvements. It is probable that some reforms, such as the extensive rewriting of the Key West accord, would actually make matters worse. The two reforms that do offer some hope of improvement are the strengthening of joint institutions within the present military structure and the establishment of biennial budgeting. The former has already been adopted; the latter remains on the table. Biennial budgeting would bring much-needed stability to the acquisition of military systems and would focus more attention on longer-range issues of strategy and force structure; strengthening the joint capability of the officer corps offers the prospect of improvements in the conduct of operations. It goes without saying that such reforms — and the more far-reaching measures that have been considered here — would not guarantee wise choices in the great issues of war and peace the United States will confront in the coming years. They might even magnify error and deepen our predicament. But they would help restore to political deliberation and military command a measure of the "energy" that is now so sorely lacking, and such a result is not to be despised.

Conclusion

The epigraph to this work comprises two famous quotations — one from Alexander Pope, the other from Alexis de Tocqueville — that express two very different attitudes toward the whole question of institutional thought. Pope's couplet, "For the forms of government let fools contest/Whate'er is best administer'd is best," is widely known to students of American government because it is cited by Alexander Hamilton in number 68 of *The Federalist Papers*. Hamilton pronounced it a "political heresy" in which we "cannot acquiesce." But he acknowledged its kernel of truth by noting that "the true test of a good government is its aptitude and tendency to produce a good administration."[1] Its kernel of truth is equally apparent today. Students of "forms" must be careful lest they exaggerate the importance of the formal institutional arrangements of any government structure. This is particularly true of the relationship between civilians and the military. An appropriate pattern of such relations rests preeminently on the ethic each observes in its dealings with the other; beyond a certain point, no institutional arrangement can secure the observance of this ethic in practice. A comparable error arises from the tendency to attribute to institutional deformity failures that really spring from an absence of political intelligence or foresight, and much of the commentary on contemporary civil-military relations occasionally falls victim to this mistake. What organizational defects have not caused, organizational reforms will not cure; and indeed the mistaken diagnosis often gives rise to remedies that might do real harm — and at the least will certainly confuse the patient.

Tocqueville's observation on the importance of forms in a democracy is probably better known and certainly more congenial. Appearing at the end of *Democracy in America*, it summarizes a theme that runs throughout his classic work, and it indicates why he found the young republic so interesting and so profitable a subject for the student of democracy. It was Tocqueville's view that the finely balanced set of institutional arrangements devised by the Founders would enable the egalitarian impulse — which he saw sweeping the world, and which he thought contained the seeds of great danger — to be deflected and harnessed and thus made compatible with the preservation of liberty. He believed that the democratic temper so characteristic of Jacksonian America would one day reappear in France, and he despaired for the future of his own country because he feared it would lack the countervailing forces that existed in America and that determined whether the principle of equality would lead "to servitude or freedom, to knowledge or barbarism, to prosperity or wretchedness." [2]

The student of American civil-military relations cannot fail to note the irony that many of the checks and balances that have been so successful in preserving freedom in the United States are the same ones that make it extremely difficult to establish an appropriate pattern of civil-military relations. Samuel P. Huntington, who discussed the tension in illuminating detail in *The Soldier and the State*, could in the end offer no resolution. "Within the framework of the separation of powers" — and, he might have added, of independent military services — "institutional adjustments can be made which will reduce its deleterious effects upon civilian control. But it will never be possible to eliminate these effects completely. A lesser measure of civilian control and lower standards of military professionalism are the continuing prices the American people will have to pay for the other benefits of their constitutional system." [3] It is difficult to dissent from his conclusion. Certainly events since he wrote have not proved him wrong. The prospect of modest improvement is still there, and an imaginative political leader could no doubt grasp it. Yet the institutional reforms that are possible, combating the lack of unified direction on both sides of the civil-military divide, would almost certainly leave the essentials of the system intact.

Reflection on the importance of "forms" still has much to teach us. They "perpetually retard or arrest" individuals in some of their projects, and for this reason Tocqueville believed that "men living in democratic ages" would be hostile to them: such men "commonly aspire to none but easy and present gratifications, they rush onwards to the object of their desires, and the slightest delay exasperates them." That is, of course, the "very thing that renders forms so useful." [4] The forms that are relevant in maintaining an appropriate pattern of civil-military relations are much different from those invented by the framers of the Constitution, for they lived in an age when the idea of military professionalism was just emerging, and the institutions they erected are, as we have seen, hostile in some degree to the achievement of objective civilian control. The characteristic device of the American science of politics — to supply "by opposite and rival interests, the defect of better motives" — may have unfortunate consequences in civil-military relations, an appropriate pattern of which requires a measure of mutual deference on the part of both statesmen and soldiers, as each pursue their special (and overlapping) purposes.

Civilian responsibility is of a certain kind. Preeminently, it is to ensure that the force structure and operational strategies maintained by the military are in harmony with political objectives. This reconciliation of ends and means must be undertaken by civilians because there is no one else to do it (or at least to do it in a manner consistent with the principles of representative government). That this is a difficult and challenging task in itself is clear. It may at times require far-reaching civilian intervention that impinges on the autonomy of military organizations; but such interventions will be more easily effected, and less resented by the military, if they are informed by the requirements and necessities of high policy. Our military officers understand this precept, and they have in the end always been willing to subordinate themselves to political direction, even when they thought it slightly foolish. This feature of the American officer corps is not to be lightly dismissed or taken for granted.

Civilians also have the primary responsibility for ensuring that the military efficiently procures the vast range of goods and services it consumes. The expertise required is that of the business executive. This is necessarily a subsidiary role: efficiency means nothing unless it supports military effectiveness (just as operational excellence is of little value unless it is harnessed to support sensible political objectives). The method, as Mahan said, exists for the result. Military officers, moreover, necessarily play a critical role in efficient procurement; in this area, at least, "fusionism" is an inescapable fact of life. But primary responsibility for ensuring that the administrative business of the military establishment is efficiently managed nevertheless belongs to civilian officials at the Department of Defense, and here there is considerable room for improvement. Perhaps the most important step in effecting such improvement is an indirect one. It lies in the alteration of the political process by which the executive and legislative branches now pass upon military requests. Two-year budget plans and a reduction in congressional review would not remove military procurement from all the political pressures that today complicate the achievement of managerial efficiency at the Department of Defense. Nor, in the end, should they. But they would improve business efficiency without seriously compromising military effectiveness or political control and could make a real difference at the margin.

Forcing change on the military in those matters that concern its professional function raises a much different set of considerations. Here civilians ought to tread carefully. They have great destructive potential, but their power to effect enduring reform is limited. At the least, therefore, those on the outside who challenge the military's professional understanding and seek to transform it — as the military reformers do today — must meet a significant burden of proof. That, I have argued, they have not done, and in the tangle of conflicting claims we rightly defer to the expertise of the existing set of military professionals.

Whether the case of the military reformers will ever gain acceptance at the highest levels of the government, we have no way of knowing. It will depend upon the whims of the people and the fortunes of our politics, not the efforts of defense analysts. Throughout the 1980s, Gary Hart was the standard-bearer of military reform. The scandal that felled him also dealt a grievous blow to the military reformers, for his withdrawal from American political life leaves no obvious champion of reform ideas in the electoral arena. Other presidential contenders, to be sure, may embrace reform, but they are unlikely to be true believers in the reform gospel as was Senator Hart. The issues raised by the reformers are too difficult and too abstract to appeal to the ordinary run of politicians, and the lapse of his candidacy may prove fatal. Still, the reform critique is widely accepted among civilian critics, particularly in the news media. Whatever its political prospects, it is certain that we have not heard the last of it.

Even now, it remains difficult to know what strategic consequences would follow from the attempt to reorder the services along reform lines, if only because the reformers themselves have tried to separate the problems of American strategy from the tactical and operational aspects of "military reform." Yet the two levels of analysis cannot be quite so easily separated. The general opposition to the large-deck aircraft carrier and the long-range bomber would gradually yield a force structure without much striking power for a broad range of military contingencies in the Third World. So too would the rejection of precision-guided munitions. Many reformers, moreover, desire a much greater reliance on the use of reserves in American ground forces, and they often combine this with a call for a reduction of American ground forces in Europe. These military reforms would have clear strategic consequences, which in the main are undesirable. For they would weaken one of the primary pillars of deterrence in Europe — the presence of active ground forces prepared to do combat with Soviet forces at the first outbreak of a war — and they would deprive the United States of the military instruments whose use would be most consistent with the limited nature of American interests throughout the Third World.

The administrative costs of military reform would be equally harmful. The cancellation of so many different weapons systems would cause administrative disruption on a huge scale. The financial costs of closing down production lines at so many major defense plants would be substantial, with most of the money going to the lawyers rather than the skilled technical community underlying the defense industrial base. That community still does manage, for all its problems, to produce some of the best military equipment in the world. To terminate so much of it on behalf of reformers' theory of warfare is, at best, a big gamble.

These strategic consequences and administrative disruptions are enough to condemn the program. That they would be accompanied by a crisis in civil-military relations seems equally clear. For the reform critique is, in its very essence, a challenge to the professional competence and intellectual honesty of the American officer corps. Those few officers who are receptive to reform ideas are of course exempted from this attack; for the most part, however, the indictment runs wide and deep. The justifications the services offer for their own programs are dismissed as reflecting bureaucratic habit and not professional understanding. We are asked to believe that the services have not only erred, but erred egregiously; that the professional military has not only made mistakes but constructed a view of the nature of contemporary warfare that is profoundly and systematically wrong.

The reverse, however, is closer to the truth. Despite all the difficulties that plague the military establishment, the doctrinal proclivities of the individual services hold up reasonably well upon examination — far better, in fact, than the writings of the military reformers. The military capabilities provided by the services offer vital support for the vindication of American interests in the world — something that cannot be said for the force structure endorsed by most reformers. One important area where there did appear to be serious inadequacies — the deficiency in cross-service operational expertise — has already been addressed by Congress in its well-conceived 1986 Defense Reorganization Act. And though much remains to be done to ensure that these legislative reforms are carried out, the beginning is auspicious.

As an intellectual critique, the case of the military reformers has been provocative and lively; their brazen challenge has stimulated wide-ranging debate on virtually every aspect of American military policy. Some of their ideas, though in less extreme form, have found a receptive audience in military circles and now form part of the conventional wisdom among defense analysts, whether civilian or military. The debate has been a healthy one, and in one area in particular — the need to reduce the size and reform the internal governance of the officer corps — the reformers' case appears sufficiently strong to justify civilian intervention. If the reform critique is considered as a whole, however, it is difficult to escape the conclusion that a civilian attempt to impose the reform program on the services would issue in very serious consequences. Despite its promise, it would in fact make things worse rather than better. It is therefore to be hoped that this program never achieves political salience and that future historians will place the military reform movement in the perspective it deserves — as an always interesting, sometimes brilliant, but politically irrelevant episode in the intellectual history of American military thought.

Notes

INTRODUCTION

1. M. J. C. Vile, *Constitutionalism and the Separation of Powers* (Oxford: Clarendon Press, 1967), p. 1.
2. Cf. Huntington, *Soldier and the State*, pp. 1-2.
3. Albion, *Makers of Naval Policy*, p. 20.
4. Clausewitz, *On War*, p. 607.

CHAPTER 1. THE DIVISION OF RESPONSIBILITY

1. Clausewitz, *On War*, pp. 605-6. Clausewitz's discussion of the relation between war and policy (published in 1833) has received extensive exegetical comment. Three particularly interesting examples are Bernard Brodie, "A Guide to the Reading of *On War*," in ibid., pp. 642-46; Michael Howard, *Clausewitz* (Oxford: Oxford University Press, 1983), pp. 34-46; and Aron, *Peace and War*, pp. 21-46.
2. Huntington, *Soldier and the State*, p. 56.
3. See Brodie, *War and Politics*, pp. 81-91, 493-96. The reaction to the military dominance of security policy came earlier in Europe. See Watt, *Too Serious a Business*.
4. See, in particular, Brodie, *Strategy in the Missile Age*, pp. 21-70 (but see also p. 64); Robert Osgood, "The Evolution of Force," in *Force, Order, and Justice*, ed. Robert E. Osgood and Robert W. Tucker (Baltimore: Johns Hopkins Press, 1967), pp. 54-55; and Stephen Van Evera, "The Cult of the Offensive and the Origins of the First World War," in Miller, *Military Strategy and the Origins of the First World War*, pp. 58-107.
5. See "Editor's Introduction," in Kennedy, *War Plans of the Great Powers*, p. 19. This view of civil-military relations in 1914 does not undercut the central contention of the civilian strategists, for it was an error in principle, and something Clausewitz himself would never have approved, to believe that war strategy was a province in which civilians had no right to interfere. And indeed, Germany was to pay dearly for this widespread perception during the course of World War I, for it was this that underlay the increasing popularity and power of Hindenburg and Ludendorff, who by 1917 had virtually usurped civilian power.
6. See Posen, *Sources of Military Doctrine*, pp. 24-29, 105-6. See also the treatment by Richard Challener, *The French Theory of the Nation in Arms*,

1866-1939 (New York: Russell and Russell, 1965); Aron, *Peace and War*, pp. 40-42; and Huntington, *Common Defense*, pp. 9-10.

7. See Millis, *Arms and Men*, pp. 226-27; Weigley, *American Way of War*, p. 193; and Sprout and Sprout, *Rise of American Naval Power*.

8. Brodie, *Strategy in the Missile Age*, pp. 18-19.

9. Mahan, "The Principles of Naval Administration," pp. 5-6.

10. Roherty, *Decisions of Robert S. McNamara*, pp. 49, 53.

11. Brodie, *Strategy in the Missile Age*, p. 8.

12. On "total package procurement," see Perry et al., *System Acquisition Strategies*; on the other McNamara reforms, see the sources cited below in chap. 2, n. 21.

13. Clausewitz, *On War*, p. 624.

14. To similar effect, see Edward Luttwak, "Effectiveness and Efficiency," in Barlow, *Reforming the Military*, pp. 1-4.

15. Hart, *Strategy*, p. 335.

16. On the distinction between the level and the scope of military professionalism, see Huntington, *Soldier and the State*, pp. 86-87.

17. Hammond, *Organizing for Defense*, p. 85.

18. Leonard D. White, with the assistance of Jean Schneider, *The Republican Era, 1869-1901: A Study in Administrative History* (New York: Macmillan, 1958), p. 162. On the debate over the organization of the Navy Department, see particularly Huntington, *Soldier and the State*, pp. 186-89, 247-51; and Hammond, *Organizing for Defense*, pp. 49-84. Also of interest are Albion, *Makers of Naval Policy*; Love, *Chiefs of Naval Operations*; and Spenser Wilkinson, *The Command of the Sea and the Brain of the Navy* (Westminster: Archibald Constable, 1900).

19. On the events that lay behind American strategy in the war with Spain, see "The Influence of Strategy upon History: The Acquisition of the Philippines," in *Politics, Strategy, and American Diplomacy: Studies in Foreign Policy, 1873-1917*, by John A. S. Grenville and George Berkeley Young (New Haven: Yale University Press, 1966), pp. 267-96.

20. The passage appears in Root's 1902 report as Secretary of War, excerpted in Root, *Military and Colonial Policy of the United States*, pp. 423-24. On the Root reforms, and more generally the administration of the U.S. Army up to World War II, see Huntington, *Soldier and the State*, pp. 251-53; Hammond, *Organizing for Defense*, pp. 10-48; Weigley, "Elihu Root Reforms and the Progressive Era," pp. 11-27; Hewes, *From Root to McNamara*; Stephen Skowronek, *Building a New American State* (Cambridge: Cambridge University Press, 1982); and Mark Skinner Watson, *Chief of Staff: Prewar Plans and Preparations*, United States Army in World War II (Washington, D.C.: Government Printing Office, 1950), pp. 57-84.

21. Huntington, *Soldier and the State*, p. 144. See also Richard D. Challener, *Admirals, Generals, and American Foreign Policy, 1898-1914* (Princeton: Princeton University Press, 1973), pp. 364-65. "Nothing," Challener notes, "came of the episode."

22. For this interpretation, see particularly Hammond, *Organizing for Defense*, pp. 47-48.

23. Huntington, *Soldier and the State*, pp. 83-85.

24. Betts, *Statesmen, Soldiers, and Cold War Crises*, p. 32.

25. See Richard B. Stewart, "The Reformation of American Administrative Law," *Harvard Law Review* 88 (June 1975): 1678.

26. On "bureaucratic revisionism"—a term coined by Betts—see Allison, *Essence of Decision*; Halperin, Clapp, and Kanter, *Bureaucratic Politics and Foreign Policy*; Art, "Bureaucratic Politics and American Foreign Policy"; and Krasner, "Are Bureaucracies Important?"

27. Cited in Philip B. Kurland, *Politics, the Constitution, and the Warren Court* (Chicago: University of Chicago Press, 1970).

28. See Huntington, *Soldier and the State*, pp. 350–54; and Townshend Hoopes, "Civilian-Military Balance," *Yale Review* 43 (Winter 1954): 221–22.

29. Huntington, "Defense Organization and Military Strategy," p. 26. "Strategic planning," Huntington writes, "should not be dominated by civilian agencies."

30. See Dews, *Acquisition Policy Effectiveness*, pp. 11–17.

31. Huntington, *Soldier and the State*, pp. 186–89, 315–44.

32. On the conflict between Lloyd George, Haig, and William Robertson, see the discussion by Harvey A. De Weerd, "Churchill, Lloyd George, Clemenceau: The Emergence of the Civilian," in Earle, *Makers of Modern Strategy*, pp. 295–301; and Ropp, *War in the Modern World*, pp. 264–65. The possibility that the near catastrophe in 1918 owed more to a lack of preparation by Haig than to the failure of Lloyd George to send needed reinforcements is considered in Basil Collier, *The Lion and the Eagle: British and Anglo-American Strategy, 1900–1950* (New York: Capricorn Books, 1973), pp. 166–70.

33. See Hammond, *Organizing for Defense*, pp. 145–58, 168–70, 176–82.

34. Alexander Hamilton, James Madison, and John Jay, *The Federalist Papers*, ed. Clinton Rossiter (New York: New American Library, 1961; orig. publ. 1787–88), no. 51, p. 322.

Chapter 2. The Lack of Unified Direction

1. William Cobbett and T. C. Hansard, eds., *The Parliamentary History of England from the Earliest Period to 1803*, (London, 1806–20), 18: 1257.

2. See Robert J. Art, "Congress and the Defense Budget: Enhancing Policy Oversight," in Art, Davis, and Huntington, *Reorganizing America's Defense*, p. 412. Other numerical measures of the growth of congressional intervention may be found in Deborah M. Kyle, "Congress 'Meddled' with over Half of the DOD's FY 84 Budget Line Items," *Armed Forces Journal International*, February 1984, p. 24. See also the remarks of Senators Barry Goldwater and Sam Nunn, the first of their series of wide-ranging speeches delivered to the Senate in early October 1985, reprinted in "Defense Organization: The Need for Change," *Armed Forces Journal International*, October 1985 Extra, pp. 4–9.

3. Alexander Hamilton, James Madison, and John Jay, *The Federalist Papers*, ed. Clinton Rossiter (New York: New American Library, 1961; orig. pub. 1787–88), no. 70, p. 424.

4. Wilfred E. Binckley, *President and Congress* (New York: Vintage Books, 1962), called it the "Second Era of Good Feeling." The great power Congress has traditionally exercised over military policy is apparent from the standard histories in this area: see particularly Weigley, *History of the United States Army*; Millis, *Arms and Men*; and Albion, *Makers of Naval Policy*. The classic

analysis of the relationship between the separation of powers and civil-military relations is Huntington, *Soldier and the State*, pp. 163–64, 177–84.

5. Cited in Alistair Horne, *The Price of Glory: Verdun 1916* (New York: Penguin Books, 1964), p. 32. The perverse incentives of contemporary defense decision making (many of which result from the separation of powers) are examined in Stockfisch, *Incentives and Information Quality in Defense Management*.

6. See Mayhew, *Congress*.

7. Whether the Defense Reorganization Act will overcome these problems is considered in chapter 5.

8. Cf. the analysis in Amos Perlmutter, "Military Incompetence and Failure: A Historical, Comparative and Analytical Evaluation," *Journal of Strategic Studies* 1 (September 1978): 121–38.

9. See Gabriel, *Military Incompetence*, pp. 149–86.

10. See the account in Arthur T. Hadley, *The Straw Giant: Triumph and Failure: America's Armed Forces* (New York: Random House, 1986), pp. 3–28.

11. See Gabriel, *Military Incompetence*, pp. 117–48; and *Report of the DOD Commission on Beirut International Airport Terrorist Act, October 23, 1983* (Washington, D.C.: Government Printing Office, 1983).

12. See Summers, *On Strategy*.

13. See Lewy, *America in Vietnam*.

14. Dwight D. Eisenhower, *Public Papers of President Dwight D. Eisenhower* (Washington, D.C.: Government Printing Office, 1959).

15. Hammond, *Organizing for Defense*, p. 372; and Huntington, "Defense Organization and Military Strategy" (reprinted in Art, Davis, and Huntington, *Reorganizing America's Defense*).

16. Huntington, "Defense Organization and Military Strategy," p. 45.

17. For representative critiques of the deficiencies of the Joint Chiefs of Staff, see *Reorganization Proposals for the Joint Chiefs of Staff*. See also Brown, *Thinking about National Security*, pp. 207–14; Korb, *Joint Chiefs of Staff*, esp. pp. 94–131; and the Staff Report to the Committee on Armed Services, United States Senate, *Defense Organization: The Need for Change*, 99th Cong., 1st sess. (Washington, D.C.: Government Printing Office, 1985).

18. See Warner R. Schilling, "The Politics of National Defense: Fiscal 50," in Schilling, Hammond, and Snyder, *Strategy, Politics, and Defense Budgets*; Huntington, *Common Defense*, pp. 374–78.

19. Glenn H. Snyder, "The 'New Look' of 1953," in Schilling, Hammond, and Snyder, *Strategy, Politics, and Defense Budgets*, p. 413. See also Armacost, *Politics of Weapons Innovation*.

20. Enthoven and Smith, *How Much Is Enough?*, p. 13.

21. Murdock, *Defense Policy Formation*, p. 42. For an assessment of the McNamara changes in budgeting, see Burt, *Defence Budgeting*; Korb, "Budget Process in the Department of Defense." McNamara's view of interservice rivalry is also examined in Robert F. Coulam's excellent study, *Illusions of Choice*, esp. pp. 46–47.

22. See the perceptive analysis in Rosen, "Systems Analysis and the Quest for Rational Defense," pp. 8–9; and Kanter, *Defense Politics*, pp. 62–69.

23. Cf. Huntington, "Defense Organization and Military Strategy," p. 45; also pp. 23–24, 31–33. A similar change underlies the analysis in Halperin and Halperin, "Key West Key."

24. See Schlesinger, "Reorganizing the Joint Chiefs."
25. To similar effect, see Luttwak, "Why We Need More 'Waste, Fraud, and Mismanagement' in the Pentagon," p. 27.
26. See Huntington, *Soldier and the State*, p. 418; idem, *Common Defense*, p. 264.
27. I investigate this danger in greater detail in *The Future of American Strategy* and in "American Strategy: Past and Future," in Mandelbaum, *American Military Policy*.

Chapter 3. Some Organizational Dilemmas

1. Van Creveld, *Command in War*, p. 6.
2. White and Schneider, *Republican Era*, p. 162.
3. Luttwak and Horowitz, *Israeli Army*, p. 54.
4. Van Creveld, *Command in War*, pp. 245-46.
5. See van Creveld, *Command in War*, p. 244; and Betts, *Statesmen, Soldiers, and Cold War Crises*, pp. 13-14.
6. See Allison, *Essence of Decision*, pp. 129-32; and Betts, *Statesmen, Soldiers and Cold War Crises*, p. 10.
7. On the confusion of the objectives sought through the bombing, see the revealing memorandum of John McNaughton in *The Pentagon Papers* (Boston: Gravel Edition, n.d.), 3: 580-82, cited in Rosen, "Vietnam and the American Theory of Limited War," p. 93. On p. 96, Rosen notes the simultaneous neglect of strategy and attention to detail characteristic of those who ran the war.
8. See Huntington, *Soldier and the State*, pp. 7-18.
9. For a sophisticated analysis of the role such thinking played in the early period of American history, see Lawrence Delbert Cress, *Citizens in Arms: The Army and the Militia in American Society to the War of 1812* (Chapel Hill: University of North Carolina Press, 1982).
10. The central hypotheses of organizational theory are summarized and examined in Posen, *Sources of Military Doctrine*, chap. 2.
11. See Coulam, *Illusions of Choice*, pp. 16-18; Steinbruner, *Cybernetic Theory of Decision*, pp. 8-12; and Allison, *Essence of Decision*, chap. 3. See also Steinbruner and Carter, "Organizational and Political Dimensions of the Strategic Posture."
12. On the horse cavalry, see Katzenbach, "Horse Cavalry in the Twentieth Century." The U.S. Navy adapted reasonably well to the aircraft carrier in the interwar period, but predominant opinion still gave excessive weight to the battleship. See Weigley, *American Way of War*, pp. 249-53; and Brodie, *Sea Power in the Machine Age*, p. 433. The Royal Navy adapted less well. See Stephen Roskill, *Naval Policy between the Wars*, 2 vols, (London: Collins, 1968-76), 2: 406-12. For a balanced discussion, see Lautenschlager, "Technology and the Evolution of Naval Warfare." Whether the commanders on the Western Front deserved all the venom writers like Liddell Hart poured out on them after World War I because of their continual employment of the infantry charge is considered from different perspectives in John Terraine, "Field Marshal the Earl Haig," in *The War Lords: Military Commanders of the Twentieth Century*, ed. Michael Carver (Boston: Little, Brown, 1976), pp. 23-43; and Bond, *Liddell Hart*. On the introduction of the ICBM, see Beard, *Developing the ICBM*. On the M-16, McNaugher, *M-16 Controversies*, must be read alongside

the less solid, though more entertaining, account in Fallows, *National Defense*, pp. 76–95.

13. Alistair Buchan, "The Age of Insecurity," *Encounter* 20 (June 1963): 5, cited in Armacost, *Politics of Weapons Innovation*, p. 2. On the growing importance of technology in twentieth-century warfare, see Martin van Creveld, "Turning Points in Twentieth Century War," in *The Washington Quarterly* (Summer 1981), pp. 3–8; and Brodie, "Technological Change, Strategic Doctrine, and Political Outcomes."

14. On these episodes, see Richard G. Head, "The A-7 Decisions: A Case Study of Weapons Procurement," in *American Defense Policy*, 5th ed., ed. John F. Reichart and Steven R. Sturm (Baltimore: Johns Hopkins University Press, 1982), pp. 613–25; Coulam, *Illusions of Choice*, pp. 285–86; McNaugher, *M-16 Controversies*, pp. 103–5, 123–28.

15. See "Defense Organization: The Need for Change," *Armed Forces Journal International*, October 1985 Extra, p. 50; and Arthur J. Alexander, *The Linkage between Technology, Doctrine, and Weapons Innovation: Experimentation for Use*, P-6621 (Santa Monica, Calif.: Rand Corporation, 1981).

16. *New York Times*, 23 January 1983; *Wall Street Journal*, 5 June 1983.

17. See Alexander M. Bickel's prophetic observations on this point in *The Supreme Court and the Idea of Progress* (New York: Harper and Row, 1970), esp. pp. 173–81.

18. James Bradley Thayer, "The Origin and Scope of the American Doctrine of Constitutional Law," in *Legal Essays* (Boston: Boston Book Company, 1908), p. 39.

19. Cf. Raymond Aron, *Main Currents in Sociological Thought*. Vol. 1. *Montesquieu, Comte, Marx, Tocqueville: Sociologists and the Revolution of 1848* (New York: Basic Books, 1965), p. 21.

20. Cited in Stephen Roskill, *The Strategy of Sea Power* (London: Collins, 1962), p. 132. On this episode, see also Arthur J. Marder, *From the Dreadnought to Scapa Flow: The Royal Navy in the Fisher Era, 1904–1919*. Vol. 4. *1917: Year of Crisis* (London: Oxford University Press, 1969); Elting E. Morison, *Admiral Sims and the Modern American Navy* (New York, Russell and Russell, 1968; originally published 1942), pp. 337–63; A. Temple-Patterson, "Jellicoe," in Carver, *Lords*, pp. 10–11. Though Churchill's comment refers specifically to World War I, he often ascribed the absence in the British army on the eve of war in 1939 of a "single effective armored division or a coherent doctrine of armoured warfare" to military conservatism as well and thus to the peculiar inability of military establishments to adapt to change. As Brian Bond has recently argued, however, "it was the lack of a definite European role more than 'military conservatism' which impeded the growth of armoured divisions in the later 1930s" (*British Military Policy between the Two World Wars*, p. 8). In Britain the real failure was political, not military. See also John J. Mearsheimer's perceptive discussion, "The British Generals Talk."

21. Record, "Why America's Military Has Joined the Ranks of the Losers."

Chapter 4. The Limitations of Military Reform

1. See Kuhn, "Department of Defense," p. 109; Hart, "U.S. Senate and the Future of the Navy"; and Lind, "Is It Time to Sink the Surface Navy?" Similar in many respects to Senator Hart's position is that of Admiral Stansfield Turner,

"Thinking about the Future of the Navy," and Turner and Thibault, "Preparing for the Unexpected."

2. See Pierre M. Sprey, "Land-Based Tactical Aviation," in Barlow, *Reforming the Military*, pp. 35–40; Canby, "General Purpose Forces"; idem, "The Interdiction Mission."

3. See Steven L. Canby, "The Army," in Barlow, *Reforming the Military*, pp. 29–33; Hart, "Military Reform Budget"; Lind, "FM 100-5," p. 58. See also John J. Fialka, "Army Shifts Strategy to Give Small Units Room to Maneuver," *Wall Street Journal*, 22 January 1982.

4. See Canby, "Military Reform and the Act of War"; idem, "NATO"; and Canby and Dorfer, "More Troops, Fewer Missiles," p. 14. See also Luttwak, "American Style of Warfare and the Military Balance," and idem, "Operational Level of War."

5. See Record, *Rapid Deployment Force and U.S. Military Intervention in the Persian Gulf*, a second edition of which was published in 1983. See also by Record, "Is the Pentagon Kidding?" William Lind has also written extensively in favor of vesting the RDF mission in the Marine Corps. See Barlow, *Reforming the Military*, pp. 25–28. The concept of operations he envisages for the Corps is spelled out in Lind, "Defining Maneuver Warfare for the Marine Corps," and idem, "Proposing Some New Models for Marine Mechanized Units." Record and Lind coauthored a piece in 1978, "Twilight for the Corps?" setting forth many of these same ideas. Others who have embraced the proposal to vest the RDF mission in the Marine Corps include Alan Ned Sabrosky, "The United States Marine Corps," in Bonds, *U.S. War Machine*, pp. 206–19; Philip L. Bolte, "It's Time to Assign One of Two Missions to Each of the US' Two Large 'Armies,'" *Armed Forces Journal International*, January 1982, pp. 65–68; and Luttwak, "Why We Need More 'Waste, Fraud, and Mismanagement' in the Pentagon," p. 27.

6. See Pierre Sprey, "The Case for Better and Cheaper Weapons," in Clark et al., *Defense Reform Debate*, pp. 193–208.

7. See Luttwak, *Pentagon and the Art of War*, idem, "New Arms Race?" Record, "Fortunes of War"; and Lind, "Military Doctrine, Force Structure, and the Defense Decision-Making Process."

8. In *National Defense*, James Fallows calls for a "larger, well-trained army" and a return of the draft (p. 174). In a similar vein, George Kuhn sharply criticized the failure of the Reagan administration to increase "force structure," and it seems clear from the tenor of his remarks that he favors a much larger army than the United States currently maintains (in *Agenda '83*, ed. Holwill, pp. 69, 76–78, 111–12). Senator Hart, on the other hand, has noted that if the U.S. Army were to reduce its division slice from over 40,000 to 25,000 "we could field our current 19 division equivalents with 475,000 men, a saving of about 300,000" ("Additional Views of Mr. Hart," Authorizing Appropriations for Fiscal Year 1981 . . . , Report 96-826 of the Senate Armed Services Committee, pp. 207–8). In his 1978 White Paper of Defense, Hart proposed reducing the size of the U.S. Army in Europe by 80,000 men (Hart, Taft, and Lind, *White Paper on Defense*, pp. 68–71). Cf. also the argument of Jeffrey Record, "Beyond NATO: New Military Directions for the United States," in Record and Hanks, *U.S. Strategy at the Crossroads*, with that of Luttwak, *Pentagon and the Art of War*, pp. 252–65.

9. This contradiction is internal to Canby's position, a point noted by Paul A.

Dyster, "The Defense of Europe: New Variations on an Old Theme," in Mandelbaum, *American Military Policy*.

10. Cf. Lind, "Is It Time to Sink the Surface Navy?" with Turner and Thibault, "Preparing for the Unexpected," p. 125.

11. See Record, "Military Reform Caucus," which is the best overview of the caucus's activities. See also William S. Lind, "Defense Reform: A Reappraisal," in Clark et al., *Defense Reform Debate*, p. 332. Lind and Record coauthored a scathing piece on the Marine Corps in August 1985 in the *Washington Post*, indicating that their initial hopes that the Corps would prove receptive to reform influence were mistaken. The Air Force has also been moving in a direction opposite that urged by the reformers since its acceptance (under the influence of Boyd and Sprey) of the F-16 in the early 1970s. Only in the Army has there been much acceptance of reform themes, but it has thus far been mostly a doctrinal acceptance and has not affected the Army's procurement program.

12. Cf. Samuel P. Huntington, "Foreword," in Clark et al., *Defense Reform Debate*, pp. ix–x.

13. Rosen, "Systems Analysis and the Quest for a Rational Defense."

14. See Canby, "Army," in Barlow, *Reforming the Military*, p. 31; Luttwak, "New Arms Race?" Lewy, *American in Vietnam*, pp. 153–61 (who notes the existence of contributing factors only marginally related to personnel turbulence, particularly the crisis in race relations); Cohen, *Citizens and Soldiers*, pp. 102–7; and van Creveld, *Fighting Power*, esp. pp. 62–79.

15. For an instructive analysis of "readiness" and of the other requirements it must compete with, see Betts, "Conventional Forces." The two Spinney reports of 1979–80 and 1983 are examined in the valuable work of Kross, *Military Reform*, esp. chap. 3 and pp. 190–95, 200.

16. Brodie, *War and Politics*, p. 465.

17. For a general consideration of the theme, see Michael I. Handel, "Numbers Do Count: The Question of Quality versus Quantity," in Huntington, *Strategic Imperative*, pp. 193–228; Betts, "Conventional Strategy," pp. 159–62; Perry, "Fallows' Fallacies," pp. 174–82; Fallows, *National Defense*, pp. 35–75; and Kross, *Military Reform*, pp. 212–13. For excellent examinations of the debate, see Lambeth, "Pitfalls in Force Planning," and Lewis, "On the Appropriate Use of Technology."

18. See Canby, "Army," in Barlow, *Reforming the Military*, p. 30; Lind, "FM 100-5: Some Doctrinal Questions," p. 58; Fallows, *National Defense*, p. 27; and Luttwak, "American Style of Warfare," p. 57. The new field manual 100-5 published by the U.S. Army in 1982 goes a long way toward meeting many of these concerns. Yet serious doubt must persist over the significance of the doctrinal change, for two reasons: one is that the 1982 FM 100-5 also supports the notion of "using interdiction and deep attack to isolate the forward defenses," an objective the reformers believe is fundamentally contrary to the basic principles of maneuver warfare. (See de Czege and Holder, "New FM 100-5," pp. 54, 62, 67; and Record, "NATO's Forward Defense and Striking Deep," pp. 44–46.) The second reason is that U.S. forces form only a part of the NATO defense line on the Central Front. NATO forces, under current concepts, would still be deployed in linear fashion along the inter-German border in the event of war, a deployment characterized by relatively few operational reserves and, according to the reformers, vulnerable to Soviet breakthrough operations.

19. See Luttwak, "Operational Level of War," p. 79; and Joffe, "Should

NATO Go Conventional?" I consider the balance of power in Europe and the various proposals to reform NATO in greater detail in *The Future of American Strategy*, chap. 2.

20. See two works by Betts, *Surprise Attack*, pp. 176–77, and "Conventional Deterrence." The importance of rapid mobilization and the adverse military consequences of "trading space for time" are emphasized in Karber, "Strategy" pp. 37, 40. The mobile defense concept is criticized in Mearsheimer, "Maneuver, Mobile Defense, and the NATO Central Front." The case for a strategy of "conventional retaliation" has been best made not by the reformers but by Samuel P. Huntington, "The Renewal of Strategy," in Huntington, *Strategic Imperative*, pp. 22–32; and idem, "Conventional Deterrence and Conventional Retaliation in Europe."

21. Cf. John J. Mearsheimer, *Conventional Deterrence* (Ithaca: Cornell University Press, 1983). The analysis in the text assumes that the Soviet Union does in fact occupy a position of material superiority in Europe. But even if we concede conventional primacy to the Soviet Union in Europe, as the reformers have so readily done, NATO retains a plausible concept of operations in the short war. In the long war, moreover, the overall resources of the West are superior to those of the Communist bloc. It will not do to argue, as Luttwak does in *Pentagon and the Art of War* (p. 267), that the Soviet Union "has the nuclear weapons to cut short any belated wartime reconstruction of American military power." At the least, it could not do so without laying itself open to an equally devastating counterattack. It involves a radical depreciation of the deterrent power of nuclear weapons to believe that they are not sufficient to constitute a shield behind which the United States might mobilize in a long war. Whatever the merit of the contention, moreover, it represents an equally radical reversal of the position Luttwak took in "How to Think about Nuclear War." There he defended the "architecture of nuclear deterrence which is now in place" against those who sought to undermine it. But if those weapons are capable of deterring a Soviet conventional attack on Western Europe, as Luttwak once argued, why would they be incapable of deterring a nuclear attack aimed at the economic and industrial infrastructure of the United States?

22. See Canby, "Military Reform and the Art of War," pp. 121–23; and Hamilton, "Redressing the Conventional Balance."

23. Gary Hart, "Military Reform Budget for FY 1984"; see also his "Options for Action of the FY 1983 Defense Budget for the Military Reform Caucus."

24. Hart, "Military Reform Budget," pp. 13–15; see also William Boly, "The $13 Billion Dud," *California Magazine*, February 1983, and two pieces by Gregg Easterbrook, "All Aboard Air Oblivion," and "Divad." (All are reprinted in Dina Rasor, ed., *More Bucks, Less Bang: How the Pentagon Buys Ineffective Weapons* (Washington, D.C.: Fund for Constitutional Government, 1983.)

25. This claim is advanced in Halperin and Halperin, "Key West Key," pp. 117–20. Even less persuasive is the Halperins' contention that fixed-wing aircraft are superior to rotary aircraft in tactical airlift. The DOD regulations governing the allocation of roles between the Air Force and the Army in aviation are reprinted, with explanatory introductions, in Cole et al., *Department of Defense*, pp. 306–15, 330–31.

26. Cf. Luttwak, "Why We Need More 'Waste, Fraud, and Mismanagement' in the Pentagon."

27. See VISTA 1999 Task Force, *VISTA 1999: A Long Range Look at the Future of the Army and Air National Guard*, submitted to Lt. Gen. LaVern E.

Weber, Chief, National Guard Bureau, March 1982. Proposals to "modernize existing U.S. Reserve ground and tactical air units, increase their training, and provide them with war stocks" are a regular feature of William W. Kaufmann's reports for the Brookings Institution. See, e.g., Joseph A. Pechman, ed., *Setting National Priorities: The 1984 Budget* (Washington, D.C.: Brookings Institution, 1983), p. 67. The most intriguing variation on this theme is Eliot Cohen's suggested revival of a universal militia draft, whose units would prepare themselves for a "big war" with the Soviet Union in Central Europe. This in turn would allow present active Army and Marine forces to be both reduced in size and reoriented to the "small war" in the Third World. See Cohen, *Citizens and Soldiers*, pp. 186–87.

28. I consider this question at greater length in *The Future of American Strategy*.

29. Clausewitz, *On War*, p. 607. Similar issues are raised by the reform proposal to shift primary responsibility for the rapid-deployment mission to the Marine Corps (see above, note 5). The proposal is defective on a number of counts. In the first place, American air power would be of fundamental significance in contending with a Soviet invasion of Iran or an Iranian attack on the southern shore of the Gulf. Yet Marine fighter wings (although they are receiving AV-8Bs and F-18s, both aircraft of limited range) have no E-3A AWACS early-warning aircraft, no F-15s, no F-111s, and no A-10s. Second, the reformers, in arguing for an RDF composed of the Marine Corps, placed great emphasis on the current RDF's lack of forcible-entry capability. But some of the Army units that would have been eliminated from the RDF, particularly the Eighty-second Airborne Division and various Ranger units, have such a capability as well, and it would have been peculiar for the architects of the RDF, in 1980, to have eliminated these units from the purview of the force planner. The expansion of amphibious lift assets (Record proposed doubling such assets sufficient to move 2.33 Marine Amphibious Forces) could not have been completed until the early 1990s, given the obsolescence in the 1980s of many parts of the current amphibious fleet. Even then, the number of battalions that could have been kept afloat in forward-deployed positions in the Arabian Sea would have remained strictly limited.

Taking the Marine Corps as it was and is, and given the character of the security crisis in the Persian Gulf at the end of the 1970s, it was perfectly reasonable to have composed the RDF of units from all the services (though admittedly inexplicable that first the Carter and then the Reagan administration waited until 1983 before forming a unified command over these forces). Yet circumstances have changed radically in the intervening period in the Persian Gulf. The reduced salience of Persian Gulf oil in the world oil market, as I have argued elsewhere, now makes possible a strategy dispensing with ground forces entirely and relying instead on American economic and military aid and on air and naval power. See David C. Hendrickson, "The West and the Decline of Oil," *National Interest*, 1 (1985): 64–74.

30. See *Department of Defense Authorization for Appropriations for Fiscal Year 1983* (Washington, D.C.: Government Printing Office, 1982), Hearings before the Committee on Armed Services, United States Senate, 98th Cong., 1st sess., 6: 3906. And see above, note 1.

31. Hart, "Reform Budget," p. 44. Hart proposed a similar shipbuilding plan in his 1978 White Paper. In 1982 the Navy presented a study of potential light

carriers, as called for by a Hart-inspired passage in the fiscal year 1982 defense bill, which Hart says "included a ship with these characteristics." But the 44,000-ton ship described by the Navy — DESIGN 45 — did not have a variety of passive protection measures, and adding these measures to the hull would have raised the tonnage to 56,000 without increasing the thirty-eight-plane air wing. The lead ship of this 44,000-ton class was estimated by the Navy to cost $1,920 million, with follow-on ships estimated at $1,560 million (Senate Armed Services Committee, Hearings on FY 1983 Budget, 6: 3957).

In addition to rescinding the funding for the two *Nimitz*-class carriers authorized in FY 1983 and proposing the procurement of a new class of smaller carriers, the Hart budget proposed rescinding the funding for battleship activation approved in FY 1983, deferring funding for three AEGIS (CG-47)-class cruisers, and canceling the Navy's new destroyer program, the DDG-51, and the Fleet Oilers (TAO) program. Hart also recommended canceling the F-18 program and suggested though did not recommend eliminating Marine Corps fighter aviation and restructuring the carrier air wing by reducing the role of attack aircraft and placing "more emphasis on anti-air and anti-submarine warfare."

32. Hart and Lind, *America Can Win*, pp. 101–5.

33. Hart, "Reform Budget," p. 20; Senate Armed Services Committee, Hearings on FY 1983 Budget, 2: 1128.

34. Turner and Thibault, "Preparing for the Unexpected," p. 129. It may be noted parenthetically that this estimate of the future in aerial warfare is far removed from the estimate made by the reformers of land-based tactical aviation.

35. It is important to recognize that the issue is not two sided. In some potential theaters — for example, the North Atlantic and Northeast Asia — land-based aircraft and early-warning systems could provide a great deal of fighter support, and thus to the controversy over the future of sea-based air power must be added an older and different competition between the adherents of sea-based and land-based air power. This issue is examined from different perspectives in Zakheim, *U.S. Sea Control Mission*, and in Lehman, *Aircraft Carriers*, pp. 35–38. Most of the V/STOL advocates, however, tend to have a high opinion of sea-based air power. For the controversies over V/STOL, see David C. Hazen, "Breaking V/STOL Free of Catch 22," *Astronautics and Aeronautics*, March 1980, pp. 24–30; G. G. O'Rourke, "V/STOL and the U.S. Navy," *Marine Corps Gazette*, January 1979, pp. 43–47.

36. Kuhn, "Department of Defense," p. 109.

37. The reformers, as noted earlier, have also criticized the Navy's emphasis on nuclear-powered attack submarines and proposed procuring diesel-powered attack submarines suitable for barrier operations. Insofar as this involves the relatively straightforward question of "sea control," the Navy's case for the nuclear-powered attack submarine appears plausible. Our allies are equipped with diesel submarines that can perform the missions the reformers desire (for instance, in the Baltic and along the Greenland-Iceland-United Kingdom gap). The Navy also has mines available that can be placed along these choke points and launched from submarines, surface ships, and aircraft. See Byron, "Diesel Boats Forever," and Norman Freidman, *U.S. Naval Weapons* (Annapolis, Md.: Naval Institute Press, 1982), p. 114. The questionable aspect of the attack submarine program arises from the role such submarines might play in northern waters if used against the Soviet Union's force of strategic ballistic-missile sub-

marines. The Navy clearly intends to employ its attack submarines as part of a "damage limitation" strategy that aims to change, even in a conventional war, "the nuclear correlation of forces." See James D. Watkins, "The Maritime Strategy," *United States Naval Institute Proceedings*, January 1986, p. 14. Whatever the merits of this plan — and they are questionable — it raises an issue of nuclear strategy on which civilians must have the last word, and therefore a redirection of the attack submarine program on these grounds would be in no way inconsistent with the theory of civil-military relations advanced in this work. I discuss the merits of a damage-limitation strategy at length in *The Future of American Strategy*. See also, on this point, Posen, "Inadvertent Nuclear War?" pp. 28–54.

38. For the debate over the utility of air interdiction, see Canby, "Tactical Air Power in Armored Warfare." See also Myers, "Deep-Strike Interdiction," and Dews and Kozaczka, *Air Interdiction*. These works should be read in conjunction with Van Creveld, *Supplying War*, esp. pp. 231–37, and idem, "Supplying an Army," pp. 56–63.

39. *Report of Secretary of Defense James R. Schlesinger to the Congress on the FY 1976 and Transition Budgets* . . . (Washington, D.C., 5 February 1975), III-19.

40. On "organizational essence," see Halperin, *Bureaucratic Politics and Foreign Policy*, chap. 3.

41. Hart, "Reform Budget," p. 27. On the development of the F-16, see Fallows, *National Defense*, pp. 95–106, and Smith, *Use of Prototypes*, pp. 84–124.

42. See Pierre Sprey, "Land-Based Tactical Aviation," in Barlow, *Reforming the Military*, p. 36; idem, "Mach 2, Reality or Myth?" See also Sprey and Merritt, "Negative Marginal Returns in Weapons Acquisition."

43. See Lambeth, "Pitfalls in Force Planning," p. 109. Lambeth is careful not to condemn LANTIRN (Low-Altitude Navigation and Targeting Infrared for Night) entirely. But he persuasively argues that a "more operationally oriented approach might have concentrated on nearer-term development of just the navigation pod and *some* discrimination capability in the targeting pod, while deferring work on the more exotic target-recognition features until the requisite technology was farther along." Hart, in his "Military Reform Budget," proposes the complete cancellation of the LANTIRN program.

44. See Carus, "Bekka Valley Campaign," p. 38; and Kross, *Military Reform*, p. 188. For a broader consideration of the role of air power since 1945, see the analysis in Armitage and Mason, *Air Power in the Nuclear Age*. For a careful review of future prospects, see Neville Brown, *The Future of Air Power* (New York: Holmes and Meier, 1986).

45. The best case for the A-10 is a study by Jeffrey G. Barlow, "Close Air Support and the Soviet Threat," in *Backgrounder No. 203* (Washington, D.C.: Heritage Foundation, 1982). Barlow supported restoring the total A-10 buy to 825 aircraft and proposed a follow-on similar to the aircraft proposed by Pierre Sprey in an earlier study for the Heritage Foundation, "Land-Based Tactical Aviation," pp. 35–40. The Hart reform budget contained no funds for procuring additional A-10s but proposed instead the development of a follow-on aircraft with characteristics similar to those urged by Sprey and Barlow.

46. This ought not to preclude serious consideration of a follow-on to the

A-10, perhaps incorporating many of the features of the Combined Arms Fighter proposed by Sprey. The relevant comparison is not only with multimission aircraft like the F-16 but also with the Army's attack helicopters. This is a problem where the cross-service expertise of a strengthened Joint Staff, considered below, would be particularly useful.

47. William S. Lind, "Defense Reform: A Reappraisal," in Clark et al., *Defense Reform Debate*, p. 333.

48. For a balanced assessment, see Norman Friedman, "Elmo Russell Zumwalt, Jr.," in Love, *Chiefs of Naval Operations*, pp. 365–79.

49. Record, "Why America's Military Has Joined the Ranks of the Losers."

CHAPTER 5. THE QUESTION OF INSTITUTIONAL REFORM

1. See David C. Jones, "What's Wrong with the Defense Establishment?" in Clark et al., *Defense Reform Debate*, pp. 272–86; Meyer, "The JCS — How Much Reform Is Needed?" and "Defense Organization: The Need for Change," *Armed Forces Journal International*, October 1985 Extra. See also Blechman and Lynn, *Toward a More Effective Defense*, and Huntington, "Defense Organization and Military Strategy" (reprinted in the excellent compendium of essays by Art, Davis, and Huntington, *Reorganizing America's Defense*). Apparently because of the opposition of Secretary of the Navy John Lehman, the Heritage report was never formally published.

2. See Serig, "Stretching the Fleet into the 1990s," pp. 168–70.

3. See the discussion in Gansler, "Reforming the Defense Budget Process." See also Vincent Puritano, "Resource Allocation in the Pentagon," Philip Odeen, "A Critique of the PPB System," Jacques S. Gansler, "How to Improve the Acquisition of Weapons," and Robert J. Art, "Congress and the Defense Budget: Enhancing Policy Oversight," all in Art, Davis, and Huntington, *Reorganizing America's Defense*. And see the perceptive analysis of Owens, "Congress' Role in Defense Mismanagement," pp. 92–96.

4. Stockfisch, "Removing the Pentagon's Perverse Budget Incentives." The Blue Ribbon Commission on Defense Management, chaired by David Packard, also supported a reduction in congressional review of line items.

5. Huntington, "Defense Organization and Military Strategy," pp. 35–38. Congress, in the Goldwater-Nichols Act of 1986, did not adopt Huntington's suggestion. Indeed, its creation of the office of the Under Secretary of Defense for Acquisition increased the functional character of the department's organization. Congress did call, however, for a series of reports from both the Secretary of Defense and the Joint Chiefs of Staff regarding the desirability of the reforms suggested by Huntington.

6. If a Secretary of Defense believes that his capacity to direct the work of the Pentagon would be furthered by such a change, he deserves the authority to make it — though to avoid disturbing the relationship with the State Department, it would be best to create three assistant secretaries responsible to the Under Secretary of Defense and charged with supervising the three mission areas (as the Georgetown study proposed). But if the Secretary of Defense is not convinced of the wisdom of such changes, as Caspar Weinberger is not, there is little reason for thinking they would improve his capacity to make wise decisions.

7. See Lynn and Posen, "Case for JCS Reform," pp. 94–95.

8. Halperin and Halperin, "Key West Key," pp. 116–17.

9. Ibid., p. 129. On "organizational essence," see Halperin, Clapp, and Kanter, *Bureaucratic Politics and Foreign Policy*, pp. 26–62.

10. See "An Evaluation of the Shallow Underwater Missile (SUM) Concept," prepared by the Office of the Deputy Under Secretary of Defense for Research and Engineering (Strategic and Space Systems), 9 April 1980; and Colin S. Gray, *The Future of the Land-Based Missile Forces*, Adelphi Paper no. 140 (London: International Institute for Strategic Studies, 1977).

11. See Lynn and Posen, "JCS Reform," pp. 90–92.

12. Luttwak, *Pentagon and the Art of War*, pp. 272–75.

13. Dwight D. Eisenhower, *Public Papers of President Dwight D. Eisenhower*, (Washington, D.C.: Government Printing Office, 1959), pp. 352–53.

14. Goldwater-Nichols Act, sec. 153.

15. Clausewitz, *On War*, p. 605.

16. See the discussion in Lynn and Posen, "JCS Reform," pp. 87–88. The various pathologies produced by the existence of separate air, naval, and ground forces in Germany were, indeed, much more severe than those that have characterized the American defense structure.

17. See Betts, *Statesmen, Soldiers, and Cold War Crises*.

Conclusion

1. Alexander Hamilton, James Madison, and John Jay, *The Federalist Papers*, ed. Clinton Rossiter (New York: New American Library, 1961; orig. pub. 1787–88), p. 414.

2. Alexis de Tocqueville, *Democracy in America*, ed. Phillips Bradley, 2 vols. (New York: Vintage Books, 1945), 2: 352.

3. Huntington, *Soldier and the State*, p. 192.

4. Tocqueville, *Democracy in America*, 2: 344.

Select Bibliography

Albion, Robert Greenhalgh. *Makers of Naval Policy, 1798–1947.* Edited by Rowena Reed. Annapolis: Naval Institute Press, 1980.

Allison, Graham. *Essence of Decision: Explaining the Cuban Missile Crisis.* Boston: Little, Brown, 1971.

Armacost, Michael. *The Politics of Weapons Innovation: The Thor-Jupiter Controversy.* New York: Columbia University Press, 1969.

Armitage, M. J., and R. A. Mason. *Air Power in the Nuclear Age.* 2d ed. Urbana: University of Illinois Press, 1984.

Aron, Raymond. *Peace and War: A Theory of International Relations.* Translated by Richard Howard and Annette Baker Fox. New York: Praeger, 1967.

Art, Robert J. "Bureaucratic Politics and American Foreign Policy: A Critique." *Policy Sciences* 4 (December 1973): 467–90.

Art, Robert J., and Vincent Davis, with Samuel P. Huntington, eds. *Reorganizing America's Defense: Leadership in War and Peace.* Washington, D.C.: Pergamon/Brassey's, 1985.

Barlow, Jeffrey G., ed. *Reforming the Military.* Washington, D.C.: Heritage Foundation, 1981.

Beard, Edmund. *Developing the ICBM: A Study in Bureaucratic Politics.* New York: Columbia University Press, 1976.

Betts, Richard K. "Conventional Deterrence: Predictive Uncertainty and Policy Confidence." *World Politics,* January 1985, pp. 153–79.

———. "Conventional Forces: What Price Readiness?" *Survival,* January/February 1983, pp. 25–34.

———. "Conventional Strategy: New Critics, Old Choices." *International Security,* Spring 1983, pp. 140–62.

———. *Statesmen, Soldiers, and Cold War Crises.* Cambridge: Harvard University Press, 1977.

———. *Surprise Attack: Lessons for Defense Planners.* Washington, D.C.: Brookings Institution, 1982.

Blechman, Barry M., and William J. Lynn, eds. *Toward a More Effective Defense: Report of the Defense Organization Project.* Cambridge, Mass.: Ballinger, 1985.

Bond, Brian. *British Military Policy between the Two World Wars*. Oxford: Oxford University Press, 1980.
———. *Liddell Hart: A Study of His Military Thought*. New Brunswick, N.J.: Rutgers University Press, 1977.
Bonds, Ray, ed. *The U.S. War Machine: An Encyclopedia of American Military Equipment and Strategy*. New York: Crown, 1983.
Brodie, Bernard. *Sea Power in the Machine Age*. Princeton: Princeton University Press, 1941.
———. *Strategy in the Missile Age*. Santa Monica, Calif: Rand Corporation, 1959.
———. "Technological Change, Strategic Doctrine, and Political Outcomes." In *Historical Dimensions of National Security Problems*, ed. Klaus Knorr, pp. 263–306. Lawrence: University of Kansas Press, 1976.
———. *War and Politics*. New York: Macmillan, 1973.
Brown, Harold. *Thinking about National Security: Defense and Foreign Policy in a Dangerous World*. Boulder, Colo.: Westview Press, 1983.
Burt, Richard. *Defence Budgeting: The British and American Cases*. Adelphi Paper 112. London: International Institute of Strategic Studies, 1974.
Byron, John L. "Diesel Boats Forever." *United States Naval Institute Proceedings*, December 1982, pp. 35–42.
Canby, Steven L. "General Purpose Forces." *International Security Review* 5 (Fall 1980): 319–46.
———. "Military Reform and the Art of War." *Survival*, May/June 1983, pp. 121–23.
———. "NATO: Reassessing the Conventional Wisdoms." *Survival*, July/August 1977, pp. 164–68.
———. "Tactical Air Power in Armored Warfare: The Divergence within NATO." *Air University Review*, May/June 1979, pp. 2–20.
Canby, Steven L., and Ingemar Dorfer. "More Troops, Fewer Missiles." *Foreign Policy*, Winter 1983/84, pp. 3–17.
Carus, W. Seth. "The Bekka Valley Campaign." *Washington Quarterly*, Autumn 1982, pp. 34–41.
Clark, Asa A., Peter W. Chiarelli, Jeffrey S. McKitrick, and James W. Reed. *The Defense Reform Debate: Issues and Analysis*. Baltimore: Johns Hopkins University Press, 1984.
Clausewitz, Carl von. *On War*. Edited and translated by Michael Howard and Peter Paret. Princeton: Princeton University Press, 1976. Originally published 1833.
Cohen, Eliot A. *Citizens and Soldiers: The Dilemmas of Military Service*. Ithaca: Cornell University Press, 1985.
Cole, Alice C., et al. *The Department of Defense: Documents on Establishment and Organization, 1944–1978*. Washington, D.C.: Office of the Secretary of Defense Historical Office, 1978.
Coulam, Robert F. *Illusions of Choice: The F-111 and the Problem of Weapons*

Acquisition Reform. Princeton: Princeton University Press, 1977.
de Czege, Huba Wass, and L. D. Holder. "The New FM 100-5." *Military Review*, July 1982, pp. 53–70.
Dews, Edmund, et al. *Acquisition Policy Effectiveness: Department of the Defense Experience in the 1970s*. Santa Monica, Calif.: Rand Corporation, 1979.
Dews, Edmund, and Felix Kozaczka. *Air Interdiction: Lessons from Past Campaigns*. N-1743-PA&E. Santa Monica, Calif.: Rand Corporation, 1981.
Earle, Edward Mead, and Gordon A. Craig, with Felix Gilbert. *Makers of Modern Strategy: Military Thought from Machiavelli to Hitler*. Princeton: Princeton University Press, 1943.
Easterbrook, Gregg. "All Aboard Air Oblivion." *Washington Monthly*, September 1981, pp. 14–26.
———. "Divad." *Atlantic Monthly*, October 1982, pp. 29–39.
Enthoven, Alain C., and Wayne K. Smith. *How Much Is Enough? Shaping the Defense Program, 1961–1969*. New York: Harper and Row, 1971.
Fallows, James. *National Defense*. New York: Random House, 1981.
Gabriel, Richard A. *Military Incompetence: Why the American Military Doesn't Win*. New York: Hill and Wang, 1985.
Gansler, Jacques S. "Reforming the Defense Budget Process." *Public Interest*, Spring 1984, pp. 62–75.
Halperin, Morton, and Priscilla Clapp with Arnold Kanter. *Bureaucratic Politics and Foreign Policy*. Washington, D.C.: Brookings Institution, 1974.
Halperin, Morton, and David Halperin. "The Key West Key." *Foreign Policy*, Winter 1983–84, pp. 114–30.
Hamilton, Andrew. "Redressing the Conventional Balance: NATO's Reserve Military Manpower." *International Security*, Summer 1985, pp. 111–36.
Hammond, Paul Y. *Organizing for Defense: The American Military Establishment in the Twentieth Century*. Princeton: Princeton University Press, 1961.
Hart, B. H. Liddell. *Strategy*. 2d rev. ed. New York: Praeger, 1967.
Hart, Gary. "Address to the National War College." 10 June 1980.
———. "Authorizing Appropriations for Fiscal Year 1981." Report 96-826 of the Senate Armed Services committee.
———. "Military Reform Budget for FY 1984." Mimeographed, n.d.
———. "Options for Action on the FY 1983 Defense Budget for the Military Reform Caucus." Mimeographed, n.d.
———. "Toward a New Consensus on Defense." *Strategic Review*, Fall 1980, pp. 9–14.
———. "The U.S. Senate and the Future of the Navy." *International Security*, Spring 1978, pp. 175–94.
———. "What's Wrong with the Military?" *New York Times Magazine*, 14 February 1982, pp. 16–45.
Hart, Gary, and William S. Lind. *America Can Win: The Case for Military Reform*. Bethesda, Md.: Adler and Adler, 1986.

Hart, Gary, and Robert Taft, Jr. with William S. Lind. *White Paper on Defense, 1978 Edition: A Modern Military Strategy for the United States.* Washington, D.C., mimeographed, 15 May 1978.

Hendrickson, David C. *The Future of American Strategy.* New York: Holmes and Meier, 1987.

Hewes, James E., Jr. *From Root to McNamara: Army Organization and Administration, 1900–1963.* Washington, D.C.: Government Printing Office, 1975.

Huntington, Samuel P. *The Common Defense: Strategic Programs in National Politics.* New York: Columbia University Press, 1961.

———. "Conventional Deterrence and Conventional Retaliation in Europe." *International Security,* Winter 1983/84, pp. 32–56.

———. "Defense Organization and Military Strategy." *Public Interest,* Spring 1984, pp. 20–46.

———. *The Soldier and the State: The Theory and Politics of Civil-Military Relations.* Cambridge: Harvard University Press, Belknap Press, 1957.

———, ed. *The Strategic Imperative.* Cambridge, Mass.: Ballinger, 1982.

Joffe, Josef. "Should NATO Go Conventional?" *Washington Quarterly,* Fall 1984, pp. 136–47.

Kanter, Arnold. *Defense Politics: A Budgetary Perspective.* Chicago: University of Chicago Press, 1983.

Karber, Phillip A. "The Strategy: In Defense of Forward Defense." *Armed Forces Journal International,* May 1984, pp. 27–50.

Katzenbach, Edward L., Jr. "The Horse Cavalry in the Twentieth Century." In *The Use of Force: International Politics and Foreign Policy,* ed. Robert J. Art and Kenneth N. Waltz, pp. 277–97. Boston: Little, Brown, 1971.

Kennedy, Paul M., ed. *The War Plans of the Great Powers: 1880–1914.* Boston: Allen and Unwin, 1979.

Korb, Lawrence J. "The Budget Process in the Department of Defense." *Public Administration Review,* July/August 1977, pp. 334–46.

———. *The Joint Chiefs of Staff: The First Twenty-five Years.* Bloomington: Indiana University Press, 1976.

Krasner, Stephen K. "Are Bureaucracies Important? (or Allison Wonderland)." *Foreign Policy* 7 (Summer 1972): 159–71.

Kross, Walter. *Military Reform: The High-Tech Debate in Tactical Air Forces.* Washington, D.C.: National Defense University Press, 1985.

Kuhn, George W. S. "Department of Defense: Ending Defense Stagnation." In *Agenda '83,* ed. Richard N. Holwill, pp. 69–114. Washington, D.C.: Heritage Foundation.

Lambeth, Benjamin. "Pitfalls in Force Planning: Structuring America's Tactical Air Arm." *International Security,* Fall 1985, pp. 84–120.

Lautenschlager, Karl. "Technology and the Evolution of Naval Warfare." *International Security,* Fall 1983, pp. 3–51.

Lehman, John. *Aircraft Carriers: The Real Choices.* Washington Paper 52. Beverly Hills, Calif.: Sage, 1978.

Lewis, Kevin N. "On the Appropriate Use of Technology." *Orbis*, Summer 1983, pp. 274-84.

Lewy, Guenter. *America in Vietnam*. Oxford: Oxford University Press, 1978.

Lind, William S. "Defining Maneuver Warfare for the Marine Corps." *Marine Corps Gazette*, March 1980, pp. 55-58.

———. "FM 100-5: Some Doctrinal Questions for the United States Army." *Military Review*, March 1977, pp. 54-65.

———. "Is It Time to Sink the Surface Navy?" *United States Naval Institute Proceedings*, March 1978, pp. 62-67.

———. "Military Doctrine, Force Structure, and the Defense Decision-Making Process." *Air University Review*, May/June 1979, pp. 21-27.

———. "Proposing Some New Models for Marine Mechanized Units." *Marine Corps Gazette*, September 1978, pp. 34-38.

Lind, William S., and Jeffrey Record. "Twilight for the Corps?" *United States Naval Institute Proceedings*, July 1978, pp. 39-43.

Love, Robert William, ed. *The Chiefs of Naval Operations*. Annapolis: Naval Institute Press, 1980.

Luttwak, Edward N. "The American Style of Warfare and the Military Balance." *Survival*, March/April 1979, pp. 57-60.

———. "How to Think about Nuclear War." *Commentary*, August 1982, pp. 21-28.

———. "A New Arms Race?" *Commentary*, September 1980, pp. 27-34.

———. "The Operational Level of War." *International Security*, Spring 1981, pp. 61-79.

———. *The Pentagon and the Art of War: The Question of Military Reform*. New York: Simon and Schuster/Institute for Contemporary Studies, 1985.

———. "Why We Need More 'Waste, Fraud, and Mismanagement' in the Pentagon." *Commentary*, February 1982, pp. 17-30.

Luttwak, Edward N., and Dan Horowitz. *The Israeli Army*. London: Allen Lane, 1975.

Lynn, William J., and Barry R. Posen. "The Case for JCS Reform." *International Security*, Winter 1985-86, pp. 69-97.

McNaugher, Thomas. *The M-16 Controversies: Military Organizations and Weapons Acquisition*. New York: Praeger, 1984.

Mahan, Alfred Thayer. "The Principles of Naval Administration." In his *Naval Administration and Warfare*. Boston: Little, Brown, 1911.

Mandelbaum, Michael, ed. *American Military Policy*. New York: Holmes and Meier, 1988.

Mayhew, David R. *Congress: The Electoral Connection*. New Haven: Yale University Press, 1974.

Mearsheimer, John J. "The British Generals Talk: A Review Essay." *International Security*, Summer 1981, pp. 165-84.

———. "Maneuver, Mobile Defense, and the NATO Central Front." *International Security*, Winter 1981/82, pp. 104-33.

Meyer, Edward C. "The JCS – How Much Reform Is Needed?" *Armed Forces Journal International*, April 1982, pp. 82–90.
Meyers, Charles F., Jr. "Deep-Strike Interdiction." *United States Naval Institute Proceedings*, November 1980, pp. 47–52.
Miller, Steven, ed. *Military Strategy and the Origins of the First World War: An International Security Reader.* Princeton: Princeton University Press, 1985.
Millis, Walter. *Arms and Men: A Study in American Military History.* 1956. Rpt. ed., New Brunswick, N.J.: Rutgers University Press, 1981.
Murdock, Clark A. *Defense Policy Formation: A Comparative Analysis of the McNamara Era.* Albany: State University of New York Press, 1974.
Owens, Mackubin Thomas. "Congress' Role in Defense Mismanagement." *Armed Forces Journal International*, April 1985, pp. 98–111.
———. "The Hollow Promise of JCS Reform." *International Security*, Winter 1985–86, pp. 106–8.
Perry, William. "Fallows' Fallacies." *International Security*, Spring 1982, pp. 174–82.
Posen, Barry N. "Inadvertent Nuclear War? Escalation and NATO's Northern Flank." *International Security*, Fall 1982, pp. 28–54.
———. *The Sources of Military Doctrine: France, Britain, and Germany between the World Wars.* Ithaca: Cornell University Press, 1984.
Record, Jeffrey. "The Fortunes of War." *Harper's*, April 1980, pp. 19–23.
———. "Is the Pentagon Kidding?" *Washington Quarterly*, Summer 1981, pp. 41–51.
———. "The Military Reform Caucus." *Washington Quarterly*, Spring 1983, pp. 125–29.
———. "NATO's Forward Defense and Striking Deep." *Armed Forces Journal International*, November 1983, pp. 42–48.
———. *The Rapid Deployment Force and U.S. Military Intervention in the Persian Gulf.* Cambridge, Mass.: Institute for Foreign Policy Analysis, 1981.
———. "Why America's Military Has Joined the Ranks of the Losers." *Washington Post National Weekly Edition*, 13 February 1984.
Record, Jeffrey, and Robert Hanks. *U.S. Strategy at the Crossroads: Two Views.* Cambridge, Mass.: Institute for Foreign Policy Analysis, 1982.
Record, Jeffrey, and William Lind. "Twilight for the Corps?" *U.S. Naval Institute Proceedings*, July 1978, pp. 39–43.
Reorganization Proposals for the Joint Chiefs of Staff. Hearings before the Investigations Subcommittee of the Committee on Armed Services. House of Representatives, 97th Cong., 2d sess. Washington, D.C.: Government Printing Office, 1982.
Roherty, James M. *Decisions of Robert S. McNamara: A Study of the Role of the Secretary of Defense.* Coral Gables, Fla.: University of Miami Press, 1970.
Root, Elihu. *The Military and Colonial Policy of the United States: Addresses and Reports by Elihu Root.* Collected and edited by Robert Bacon and James Brown Scott. Cambridge: Harvard University Press, 1924.

Ropp, Theodore. *War in the Modern World.* New York: Collier, 1962.
Rosen, Stephen. "Systems Analysis and the Quest for Rational Defense." *Public Interest,* Summer 1984, pp. 3–17.
———. "Vietnam and the American Theory of Limited War." *International Security,* Fall 1982, pp. 83–113.
Schilling, Warner R., and Paul Y. Hammond, with Glenn H. Snyder. *Strategy, Politics, and Defense Budgets.* New York: Columbia University Press, 1962.
Schlesinger, James. "Reorganizing the Joint Chiefs." *Wall Street Journal,* 8 February 1984.
Serig, Howard W., Jr. "Stretching the Fleet into the 1990s." *United States Naval Institute Proceedings,* May 1984, pp. 164–79.
Smith, G. K., et al. *The Use of Prototypes in Weapon System Development.* R-2345-AF. Santa Monica, Calif.: Rand Corporation, 1981.
Sprey, Pierre. "Mach 2, Reality or Myth? The Progression of Maximum Speeds in Fighter Aircraft." *International Defense Review* 9 (1980): 1209–12.
Sprey, Pierre, and Jack Merritt. "Negative Marginal Returns in Weapons Acquisition." In *American Defense Policy,* 3d ed., ed. Richard G. Head and Ervin J. Rokke, pp. 486–95. Baltimore: Johns Hopkins University Press, 1973.
Sprout, Harold, and Margaret Sprout. *The Rise of American Naval Power, 1776–1918.* Princeton: Princeton University Press, 1939.
Steinbruner, John D. *The Cybernetic Theory of Decision: New Dimensions of Political Analysis.* Princeton: Princeton University Press, 1974.
Steinbruner, John D. and Barry Carter. "Organizational and Political Dimensions of the Strategic Posture: The Problems of Reform." *Daedalus* 104 (Summer 1975): 131–54.
Stockfisch, J. A. *Incentives and Information Quality in Defense Management.* R-1827-ARPA. Santa Monica, Calif.: Rand Corporation, 1976.
———. *Models, Data, and War: A Critique of the Study of Conventional Forces.* R-1526-PR. Santa Monica, Calif.: Rand Corporation, 1975.
———. "Removing the Pentagon's Perverse Budget Incentives." In *Backgrounder No. 360.* Washington, D.C.: Heritage Foundation.
Summers, Harry G., Jr. *On Strategy: A Critical Analysis of the Vietnam War.* Nowata, Calif.: Presidio Press, 1982.
Turner, Stansfield. "Thinking about the Future of the Navy." *United States Naval Institute Proceedings,* August 1980, pp. 66–69.
Turner, Stansfield, and George Thibault. "Preparing for the Unexpected: The Need for a New Military Strategy." *Foreign Affairs,* Fall 1982, pp. 122–35.
Van Creveld, Martin. *Command in War.* Cambridge: Harvard University Press, 1985.
———. *Fighting Power: German and U.S. Army Performance, 1939–45.* Westport, Conn.: Greenwood, 1982.
———. "Supplying an Army: A Historical View." *Journal of the Royal United Services Institution* 123, no. 2 (1978): 56–63.
———. *Supplying War: Logistics from Wallenstein to Patton.* Cambridge: Cambridge University Press, 1977.

VISTA 1999 Task Force. *VISTA 1999: A Long Range Look at the Future of the Army and Air National Guard.* Washington, D.C., 1982.

Watt, D.C. *Too Serious a Business: European Armed Forces and the Approach to the Second World War.* Berkeley and Los Angeles: University of California Press, 1975.

Weigley, Russell F. *The American Way of War: A History of United States Military Strategy and Policy.* New York: Macmillan, 1973.

―――. "The Elihu Root Reforms and the Progressive Era." In *Command and Commanders in Modern Warfare: Proceedings of the Second Military History Symposium U.S. Air Force Academy, 2–3 May 1968,* ed. William Geffen. Washington, D.C.: Government Printing Office, 1971.

―――. *History of the United States Army.* Enlarged ed. Bloomington: Indiana University Press, 1984.

Zakheim, Dov S. *The U.S. Sea Control Mission: Forces, Capabilities, and Requirements.* Washington, D.C.: Congressional Budget Office, 1977.

Index

Administration: civilian and military responsibilities in business, 14–17, 21–27, 121; distinguished from business administration, 23; theory of, 23–24. *See also* Administrative reform

Administrative reform, 3–4; and biennial budgeting, 30, 34, 101, 102–3, 117, 121; and competition in procurement, 3–4, 16, 42; expertise required in, 14–15, 121; under Robert McNamara, 15–16, 39–40; and operational testing, 3, 16–17n, 50, 53, 80–81; and David Packard, 16, 16–17n, 25–26, 101; and postwar defense organization, 14–16; and reduction of congressional review, 103–5, 121; and reduction of staff, 72–73, 73n, 124; and "revolving door," 3; and U.S. Army, 17–18, 20–22, 27; and U.S. Navy, 17–19, 27. *See also* Duplication

Air Defense Command (ADC), 34

Air Force, U.S.: and airlift, 39–41, 108–9; and close air support, 40, 95–96, 109; and duplication, 41–42; and fighter aircraft, 2, 4, 64, 93–95; and manned bomber, 2, 44, 64, 91–93; and nuclear missions, 38–39, 51, 109–10; reform critique of, 2, 64–66, 68, 74, 91–96. *See also* Weapons systems and military programs

Army, U.S.: active vs. reserve forces in, 82–85; and airmobility, 54; and attrition style of warfare, 2–3, 64–65, 75–78; Chief of Staff for, 17–18, 20–22, 57, 109; foundation of professionalism in, 17–18, 20–22; and Robert McNamara, 53–54; organization of, in World War II, 21, 37; personnel policies of, 72–73; procurement program of, 80–82; and rapid deployment, 39–41, 83, 108–9; reform critique of, 2–3, 5, 64–65, 67–69, 75–78, 80–82; and Root reforms, 17–18, 20–22, 57; strategic utility of, 7, 75–85, 122–23. *See also* Officer Corps, U.S.; Wars and military engagements; Weapons systems and military programs

Asquith, Henry, 33

Betts, Richard, 23, 54, 72n
Blue Ribbon Commission on Defense Management (1986), 16n, 101
Bond, Brian, 130n
Boyd, John, 93
Bradley, Omar, 12
Brandeis, Louis, 58
Brodie, Bernard, 14, 15, 72n, 74
Brown, Harold, 40, 109, 110
Budgeting. *See* Administrative reform; Congress
Bureaucratic revisionists, 23
Burke, Edmund, 29–30

Canby, Steven, 63n, 65–66, 68n, 79
Carter, Jimmy, administration of, 41, 56, 102; rejection of MX plan by, 110; underfunding of force structure by, 106
Carus, W. Seth, 95
Center for Strategic and International Studies (CSIS), 100
Churchill, Winston, 59, 130n
Civil Aeronautics Board, 23
Civil-military relations, American: central issue in, 56–57; centralization vs.

147

Civil-military relations *(continued)*
  decentralization in, 46–49, 98; and
  division of military authority, 29–30,
  34–45, 100–102, 105–17, 120, 123;
  ethical vs. institutional criteria in,
  26–28, 56–59, 119, 120–21; expertise
  and innovation in, 49–57; fusionism in,
  23–24, 29, 121; greatest conundrums
  of, 59; level and scope of military professionalism in, 17–18, 21, 24–26,
  114–16, 121–22, 126n; and military
  reform, 5–6, 57–69, 97–99, 123; purposive vs. functional organization in,
  46, 105–7; and separation of powers,
  29–34, 42–43, 55, 97–98, 102–5, 120;
  unity of, 29–30, 120
Clausewitz, Carl von, 7, 11, 14, 36,
  85, 115, 125n
Cohen, Eliot A., 72n, 83, 134n
Combined Chiefs of Staff, 27
Congress, U.S.: constitutional powers of,
  30–32; and defense reorganization, 2–3,
  42, 100–101, 105–7, 111–17, 123; and
  military reform, 5, 55, 97; relations
  between Reagan administration and,
  32, 43; role of, in defense budgeting,
  3–4, 29–34, 41, 43–44, 97, 100–105,
  117, 121
Constitution, U.S., 23, 31, 102
Courter, Jim, 5
Cranston, Alan, 33
Crevald, Martin van, 46, 48
Crowe, William, 107
Cyert, Richard, 52n

Daniels, Josephus, 19
Defense, Department of: administration
  of, 3–4, 15–16, 30–34, 39–40, 42,
  44–45, 100–105, 116–17, 121, 123;
  organization of, 2–3, 30, 34–42, 44–45,
  100–102, 105–17. *See also* Administrative reform; Organizational
  reform
Defense General Staff. *See* Joint Chiefs
  of Staff
Defense Reorganization Act (1958), 37,
  40
Defense Reorganization Act (1986), 2–3,
  34, 42, 100–101, 105–7, 111–17, 123
Dewey, Admiral George, 19

Dooley, Mr., 102
Drinan, Robert, 33
Duplication: vs. competition, 4, 41;
  significance of, 41–43, 54–55

Easterbrook, Gregg, 70
Eastern Europe, 13, 66, 92
Eisenhower, Dwight D., administration
  of: and defense management, 15, 39,
  44–45; emphasis of, on nuclear retaliation, 40; Secretaries of Defense in, 15.
  See also Defense Reorganization Act
  (1958)
Ewell, Major General Julian J., 71n

Fallows, James, 68–69n, 70, 131n
Federal Trade Commission, 23
FM-100-5, 75, 132n
Forrestal, James, 27, 38–39, 108
France, 12, 51, 75, 80
Frankfurter, Felix, 23, 58
Frederick II of Prussia ("the Great"),
  12, 77
Friedman, Milton, 52

Gaddafi, Mu'ammar, 79
Gates, Thomas, 15
Gavin, James, 54
George, David Lloyd, 27, 59
Germany: blitzkriegs of, 68; General Staff
  of, 13, 115; and 1914, 12–13; proclivity
  of, for bold stroke, 77; submarine war-
  fare of, in World War I, 59. *See also*
  NATO
Gettysburg, 78
Gingrich, Newt, 5
Goldwater, Barry, 100
Goldwater-Nichols Defense Reorganiza-
  tion Act. *See* Defense Reorganization
  Act (1986)
Grant, Ulysses S., 56
Great Britain: civil-military relations in,
  during World War I, 27; and Falk-
  lands, 55, 79, 93; intervention of, in
  1914, 13. *See also* NATO
Green Berets, 54

Haig, Douglas, 27
Halperin, Morton and David, 108–9, 111
Hamilton, Alexander, 30, 32, 119

Hammond, Paul, 18, 37
Hart, Gary, 5, 7, 63, 80–81, 85–86, 91, 94, 122, 131n, 134–35n, 136n. *See also* Military reform
Heritage Foundation, 63
Holmes, Oliver Wendell, 58
Horowitz, Dan, 47
Huntington, Samuel P., xi, 11, 22, 24–27, 37, 72n, 101, 105, 120

Institutional reform. *See* Organizational reform
Interstate Commerce Commission, 23
Iran, 35, 73, 84, 92, 113

Japan, 77–78
Jarrell, Randall, 43
Jellicoe, John, 59
Joffe, Josef, 76
Johnson, Lyndon B., administration of, 45, 49. *See also* McNamara, Robert; Wars and military engagements, Vietnam War
Joint Chiefs of Staff: critique of, 3, 36–42, 100–101, 111–17; and Korean War, 12, 38; and Robert McNamara, 39–40, 55. *See also* Defense Reorganization Act (1986)
Jones, David, 100

Kennedy, Edward, 5, 33
Kennedy, John F., administration of, 39, 40, 45. *See also* McNamara, Robert
Kennedy, Paul, 13
Key West accord (1948), 34; proposed revision of, 101, 108–11, 117
Khe Sanh, 49
King, Ernest, 27
Kross, Walter, 95
Kuhn, George, 63, 88, 131n

Laird, Melvin, 16, 40, 41
Lambeth, Benjamin, 136n
Lee, Robert E., 78
Lehman, John, 85, 102
LeMay, Curtis, 53
Libya, 84
Lincoln, Abraham, 31, 56
Lind, William, 63n, 75, 98, 131n, 132n. *See also* Hart, Gary; Military reform

Logistics Command Centers, 48
Ludendorf, Erich von, 27
Luttwak, Edward, 27, 47, 70, 73n, 112, 133n
Lynn, William, 107

MacArthur, Douglas, 12, 35
McElroy, Neil H., 15
McNamara, Robert, 2, 100; affinity between military reform and, 74–75; and centralization, 32, 34, 48–49; and inter-service rivalry, 39–41, 44, 55; and PPBS, 39–40, 103; and responsibilities of Secretary of Defense, 15–16, 25, 57–58; and systems analysis, 70–72; weapons procurements sponsored by, 53–54
Madison, James, 28, 31, 120–21
Maginot Line, 13
Mahan, Alfred Thayer, 14–15, 18–19, 26, 121
Maneuver warfare, 1, 7, 36, 75–78, 82, 84–85, 95
March, James, 52n
Marine Corps, U.S.: and Beirut, 35; and duplication, 41; and fighter aviation, 68, 135n; and military reform, 5, 66–69; and rapid deployment force, 66, 82–85, 131n, 134n
Marshall, George C., 21, 27, 56
Mayaguez, 35
Meyer, General Edward C., 56, 100
Micromanagement, 32, 34, 102. *See also* Congress, U.S.
Military professionalism: in administration (scope of), 14–26, 121; and corporateness, 49–50; and expertise, 49–57; and military reform, 5–6, 59–60, 67–70, 96–99, 122; in operations, 11–14, 17, 35–36; and responsibility, 49–50, 121; in strategy (level of), 11–14, 17–26, 114–16, 121–22
Military reform: administrative consequences of, 80, 90–91, 123; and Air Force, 2, 64–66, 68, 74, 91–96; and Army, 2–3, 5, 64–65, 67–69, 75–78, 80–82; composite picture of, 1–2, 63–67; and Congress, 5, 55, 97; consensus within, 68–70; internal disagreements within, 67–68, 68–69n; leading

Military reform (continued)
  proponents of, identified, 63n (see also names of individual reformers); and maneuver warfare, 1, 7, 36, 75–78, 82, 84–85, 95; and Marine Corps, 5, 66–69; and military professionalism, 5–6, 59–60, 67–70, 96–99, 122; and Navy, 2, 63–64, 67–69, 85–91, 98, 135–36n; positive contributions of, 70–75, 123–24; predominantly civilian character of, 5–6, 69–70, 98–99; strategic consequences of, 6–7, 77, 79–80, 82–85, 87–88, 90–91, 92–93, 96–97, 122–23. See also names of individual military services; Weapons systems and military programs
Military Reform Caucus, 69, 97
Mitterand, François, 79
Montesquieu, Charles Louis de Secondat, 59
Murdock, Clark, 39

Napoleon I of France, 12
National Guard Association, 83
National Security Act (1947), 34, 37–38
National Security Council, 106
NATO: American contribution to, 6–7, 44, 65–68, 78–80, 82–85; and close air support, 67–68, 95–96; and deep interdiction, 64, 91–93; and doctrinal debate, 75–78, 84–85; and increased European ground forces, 78–80; and naval power, 89, 135n; reform critique of, 65–68
Navy, U.S.: and attack submarines, 64, 135–36n; and battleships, 68, 87, 129n; and carrier debate, 2, 7, 63–64, 68–69n, 85–88, 97, 129n; and interservice rivalry, 38–39; and McNamara program, 53; and National Security Act (1947), 37; organizational foundations of, 17–19, 21–22, 27, 47; reform critique of, 2, 63–64, 67–69, 85–91, 98, 135–36n; Secretary of, 18–19, 27, 47, 102; significance of, in protracted conflict with the Soviet Union, 68, 89–91; and surface escorts, 2, 64, 88–91, 135n
New York Times, 55
Nicaragua, 84

Nixon, Richard M., administration of, 44, 45, 84. See also Packard, David
North Korea, 84
Nunn, Sam, 100

Officer Corps, U.S.: corporate nature of, 49–50, 55–56; excessive size of, 72–73, 124; (in)competence of, 5–6, 59–60, 67–70, 96–99, 122; loyalty of, 49–50, 121; political advice of, 115–16; warriors vs. managers in, 4. See also Joint Chiefs of Staff; names of individual military services
O'Neill, Tip, 33
Organizations, theory of: centralization vs. decentralization in, 46–49; expertise and innovation in, 46, 50–57; purposive vs. functional criteria in, 46, 105–7
Organizational reform: and defense budget process, 101–5, 117, 121; and JCS Reform, 2–3, 100–101, 111–17; leading proponents of, identified, 2–3, 100–101; and office of the Secretary of Defense, 3, 101, 105–7, 137n; and reallocation of roles and missions among services, 101, 108–11; and unified commands, 2, 105–7, 111–17. See also Congress, U.S.; Joint Chiefs of Staff

Packard, David, 16, 16n, 26, 73n, 101
Patton, George, 75
Pentagon. See Defense, Department of
Persian Gulf, 92–93, 109, 134n
Petain, Henri-Philippe, 78
Planning, Programming, and Budgeting System (PPBS), 40, 103
Pope, Alexander, viii, 119
Posen, Barry, 107
President: as Commander-in-Chief, 31; increase in power of, 32; rivalry of, with Congress, 29–34, 42–43, 55, 97–98, 102–5, 120. See also names of individual presidents

Quantitative analysis of weapons systems, 70–72
Quantity vs. quality in weapons systems, 74–75, 82

Rapid Deployment Force (RDF), 66, 82, 93
Reagan, Ronald, administration of: and decentralization, 40, 92; and defense reform, 101; growth of defense budget under, 6, 107; and nuclear weapons, 42, 109–10; and readiness crisis, 43–44, 107; and strategic pluralism, 6, 42–45, 107
Record, Jeffrey, 59–60, 63n, 66, 70, 84
Ridgeway, Matthew, 54
Rogers, Bernard, 44
Roosevelt, Franklin D., 27, 56
Roosevelt, Theodore, 31, 56
Root, Elihu, 18, 20–21, 57
Russell, Richard, 109

Schlesinger, James, 91–92, 109
Sharon, Ariel, 85
Sherman, William T., 56
Sims, William S., 19, 56, 59
South Korea, 44
Soviet Union, 38, 42, 48, 68, 78, 83
Spinney, Franklin, 63n, 73
Sprey, Pierre, 63n, 93
State Department, 30, 106, 137n
Stimson, Henry, 27
Stockfisch, Jacob, 72n, 103–4
Strategic Air Command, 34
Strategy, U.S.: active vs. reserve forces in, 83–85; attrition vs. maneuver in, 1, 75–78, 84–85 (see also Maneuver warfare); civilian and military responsibilities in, 11–14, 17–28, 29, 34, 37–45, 68–70, 111–17, 121; conventional retaliation and, 77; counterinsurgency and, 54; economic decline and, 6; in Europe, 75–84, 89–90, 91–96; impact of servicism on pluralism in, 7, 37–45, 53–55, 108–11; maritime vs. continental emphasis in, 67, 89–90; modernization, readiness, and sustainability in, 42, 45, 73–74, 114–15; in Persian Gulf, 41, 44, 84–85, 134n; under Reagan administration, 44; short war vs. long war, 83, 115; in Third World, 7, 41, 67–68, 84–85, 122–23
Supreme Court, U.S., 23
Syria, 84
Systems Analysis Office, 71

Tactical Air Command, 91
Taylor, Maxwell, 54
Thayer, James Bradley, 58
Thurow, Lester, 72n
Tocqueville, Alexis de, 119–21
Truman, Harry, administration of, 12, 34
Turner, Stansfield, 86–87

Vile, Maurice, 4
VISTA 1999 report, 83

Wall Street Journal, 55
War Department. *See* Army, U.S.
War Powers Act, 31
Wars and military engagements (in chronological order):
— Seven Years' War (1756–63), 12, 77
— War of American Independence (1776–1783), 77
— Wars of French Revolution and Napoleon (1792–1815), 12
— War of 1812 (1812–15), 31
— American Civil War (1861–65), 31, 56, 76
— Spanish-American War (1898), 19, 20, 57
— Russo-Japanese War (1904–5), 51
— World War I (1914–18): and civil-military relations, 12–13, 26–27; and military conservatism, 51, 59; and positional warfare, 64–65, 68
— World War II (1939–45): American ground forces in, 83; and civil-military relations, 21, 26–27, 37, 56; French preparations for, 13, 51, 75; German General Staff in, 115; and military conservatism, 51, 59, 130n; naval tactics in, 88; and presidential power, 31–32
— Korean War (1950–53): and civil-military relations, 12; ground forces in, 45, 83; and interservice rivalry, 38
— Bay of Pigs (1961), 35
— Cuban Missile Crisis (1962), 48–49
— Vietnam War (1965–73): Air Force role in, 92–93, 94; civilian supervision of, 48–49; and counter-insurgency, 54; disengagement from, 16, 45; and distrust of military, 1; effect of, on interventionary capabilities, 41, 109;

Wars and military engagements
— Vietnam War *(continued)*
  enemy strategy in, 36, 77; irony of quantitative methods in, 71, 71n; logistics in, 48; and M-16, 53–54; nature of failure in, 35–36, 54n, 99; personnel policies in, 65, 72, 83; and presidential power, 32
— *Mayaguez* (1975), 35
— Desert One (1980 mission to rescue American hostages), 35
— Falklands (1982), 55, 79, 93
— Lebanon (1982), 55, 85, 95
— Grenada (1983), 35, 99, 113
— Lebanon (1983), destruction of Marine compound in, 35, 99
Warsaw Pact, 2, 76, 91, 96
Washington, George, 77
Watergate, 32
Weapons systems and military programs
— Air Forces: A-1E, 96; A-4, 87; A-7, 53, 96; A-10, 33, 74, 80, 91, 96; Advanced Medium Range Air-to-Air Missile (AMRAAM), 93–94; Airborne Warning and Control System (AWACS), 95; Apache AH-64 attack helicopter, 65, 80, 81; AV-8 Harrier, 87, 88; Backfire, 88; Blackjack, 87; C-5(B), 41, 109; C-17, 109; F-4 Phantom, 53, 94; F-14 Tomcat, 87; F-15 Eagle, 2, 74, 91–95, 122; F-16 Falcon, 91–94; F-18 Hornet, 33, 88; F-20, 4; Hellfire missile, 80; Hind attack helicopter, 81; IRR Maverick, 94; LANTIRN, 94, 95, 136n; Multinational Staged Improvement Program (MSIP), 93; P-3C Orion, 87; T-46, 33; V/STOL aircraft, 64, 86, 87
— Ground Forces: AR-15 (M-16) rifle, 51, 53; Bradley infantry fighting vehicle, 65, 80, 81; COHORT program, 72; Division Air Defense gun (DIVAD), 65, 80–81, 104; "Duster" antiaircraft gun, 80; Dutch Rechstreeks Instromend Mobilisable (RIM) system, 65; horse cavalry, 51; infantry charge, 51; M-1 tank, 80, 81; M-14, 51; M-113 APC, 80; Patriot missile, 80
— Naval Forces: CG-47 *Ticonderoga*-class cruiser, 64, 89; DD-51 *Burke*-class destroyer, 64, 89; DESIGN 45, 135n; *Essex* class aircraft carrier, 87; Fast Deployment Logistics Ship, 41, 109; FFC 7 *Perry*-class frigate, 87; large-deck (*Nimitz* or *Forrestal* class) aircraft carrier, 2, 64, 85–89, 90, 122; *Los Angeles*-class attack submarine, 64, 135–36n; *Oriskany*, 87; *Saratoga*, 102; SL-7 fast sealift ship, 109; V/STOL Support Ship (VSS), 87
— Nuclear Forces: B-1B bomber, 42, 92; B-36 bomber, 38; D-5 missile, 42; division of responsibility for, 14; ICBM, 51; MX missile, 42, 108–10; Pershing II, 93; Polaris submarine, 110, 111; SS-18, 110; Shallow Underwater Missile (SUM), 109–10; in strategy of Reagan administration, 44; Thor-Jupiter dispute, 39; Trident submarine, 42, 110, 111
— quantitative analysis of, 70–72
— quantity vs. quality in, 74–75, 82
Weinberger, Caspar, 3, 40, 44, 45, 81, 110. *See also* Reagan, Ronald, administration of
Westmoreland, William, 35–36, 54, 71
Whiz kids, 53, 74. *See also* McNamara, Robert
Wilson, Charles E., 15
Wilson, Woodrow, 20–21, 31

Zumwalt Elmo, 98

About the Author
DAVID C. HENDRICKSON is assistant professor of political science at The Colorado College. He is the coauthor (with Robert Tucker) of *The Fall of the First British Empire: Origins of the War of American Independence* (available from Johns Hopkins) and *The Future of American Strategy*.

Reforming Defense

Designed by Ann Walston.

Composed by Capitol Communication Systems, Inc.,
in Paladium text and display.

Printed by Thomson-Shore, Inc.,
on 50-lb. S. D. Warren's Olde Style paper,
and bound by John H. Dekker and Sons, Inc.